POLITICS
&
EVANGELICAL
THEOLOGY

A GUIDE FOR CONCERNED CHRISTIANS &
POLITICAL PROGRESSIVES

BRIAN G. MATTSON

POLITICS & EVANGELICAL THEOLOGY: A GUIDE FOR
CONCERNED CHRISTIANS & POLITICAL PROGRESSIVES

Brian G. Mattson, B.A., M.A.R., Ph.D. (University of Aberdeen) is a theologian, speaker, and writer. He serves as Senior Scholar of Public Theology for the Center For Cultural Leadership. He lives in Billings, Montana, with his wife and two daughters.

Designed by David Dalbey.

ISBN-13: 978-1477566213

TABLE OF CONTENTS

PREFACE

Facebook has a profile option to identify political views. I have noticed people frequently describing their views as "Other" rather than the more typical identifications of conservative/liberal or Republican/Democrat. "Other" is often accompanied by taglines like, "It's complicated" or "Nobody really has it figured out, do they?" There is nothing scientific about my observations here, since I have only browsed through my own modest Friend list. I do not choose my friends based on political orientation—politics rarely, if ever, rises to the level of differentiating friends from enemies—but I do find the growing political agnosticism somewhat alarming, particularly among my evangelical Christian friends.

I do not believe that it is all that complicated.

Nor do I believe that nobody really has it figured out.

Two of my great loves happen to be two things proverbially frowned upon in polite company: religion and politics. My love of politics began in 1988. Vice President George H. W. Bush visited my small hometown of Billings, Montana, and held a campaign rally in a large airplane hangar. Following his rousing (I know: hard to believe) stump speech, I weaseled my way through the crowd, squeezed through barely-existing openings to the rope line, where, to my shock and delight, he shook my hand. I was a star struck sixth-grader.

My love of theology is far deeper. Although in my teenage years I flirted with the idea of a career in the law, theology was destined to be my vocation. It began when I read Francis Schaeffer's *He Is There and He Is Not Silent*. It was above my 14-year-old head, but that little book was my first taste of a robustly intellectual faith. It was my introduction to the idea that my religious faith had implications for how to understand everything else. Christianity suddenly was a worldview for me in a way it had not been previously.

Those two childhood events are the roots of this book. If Schaeffer was right (and he was) that Christianity is a world-and-life view, then it must be relevant to what took place in that airplane hangar one hot afternoon in an electoral backwater. Not only do I believe religion and politics mix; I believe there is no alternative. Because evangelical theology is rooted in the belief that God really speaks, that he is there and he is not silent, it must involve beliefs relevant to politics.

This book is an exploration of those beliefs.

INTRODUCTION

"God is Not a Republican!" screams the bumper sticker on the car in front of me. It is, of course, accompanied by other mini-billboards. They are invariably politically left-wing. The word "Coexist" scrawled with letters made from the world's most famous religious symbols, something about world peace, and another about saving the environment. Slogans are often helpful things. They crystalize issues in a pithy and provocative way.

That one about God not being a Republican is a particularly punchy one. I do not think it is really meant to suggest that God is a Democrat, although sometimes I'm not sure. Generally it is a complaint about the seeming identification of religion with a particular political program. More specifically, in the American political context, it is a complaint that evangelical Christians, as a very large voting bloc, tend to identify their political convictions with their religious convictions. But that actually isn't the complaint, either. It is rather that many evangelical Christians identify their *conservative* political convictions with their religious convictions.

It isn't the religion that troubles people. After all, there is a burgeoning market for religious thinkers who are politically left-wing. The left has enthusiastically embraced religious leaders like Jim Wallis and his magazine, *Sojourners*. As far as I can tell, Wallis is making a very fine living, funded in part by billionaire George Soros, himself hardly a friend of conservative politics. And what, exactly, does Wallis do? He ties politically left-wing political convictions (e.g., redistributive tax rates, welfare state) to Christianity in an effort to create a new political voting bloc in America: an "evangelical left." People with "God Is Not a Republican" bumper stickers tend to welcome Jim Wallis's brand of religion with open arms.

So, it is not really about bringing God into political discourse. It is the affront of bringing God into political discourse and *having him take the conservative side of the argument.* As the sticker itself declares, the objection is not a two-way street. It does not say, "God Is Not Politically Partisan!" It says, "God Is Not a Republican!" God-talk is cool. God-talk in support of conservative political views is not cool. This explains why when left-wing politicians give flagrantly partisan speeches in the pulpits of large, inner-city African-American churches it elicits a collective yawn from the legacy media. Yet if an evangelical pastor dares to preach on hot-button political issues, the government swiftly moves in to penalize his church.[1]

Even worse contempt is heaped on the poor conservative political candidate who talks about God. When Congresswoman Michele Bachmann, Governor Rick Perry, and former Senator Rick Santorum (all committed Christians) ran for President, *The New York Times* took it as a clear and present danger to the health of the body politic. Times Executive Editor Bill Keller wrote an opinion piece that read as though having an outspoken evangelical Christian candidate for President was some sort of dangerous, unprecedented turn of events for America.[2] He gave a list of questions about the relationship between Christianity and politics that he demanded to have answered. For the good of the country, of course.

This was interesting and, for two reasons, ironic. First, in the 2008 election cycle *The New York Times*, with Bill Keller at the helm, had almost no interest in whether black liberation theology had any political implications that might interest the American people. Much less did the *Times* demand answers. It stretches credulity to believe this is for any reason other than that Keller's preferred candidate was implicated. Barack Obama had been a member of a black liberation church for over twenty years. But Obama, being the Democrat nominee, underwent little scrutiny. The second irony is that black liberation theology, in direct contrast to evangelical theology, is purely *political* theology. It takes all the familiar words of Christianity (sin, salvation, redemption, etc.) and recasts them not as spiritual realities, but this-worldly political aims. "Salvation" for black liberation theology, as exemplified by Obama's pastor, Jeremiah Wright, is the political exaltation of marginalized people at the expense of elites. It was originally developed (as an offshoot of Latin American liberation theology) as a self-consciously Marxist theology and, for Obama's pastor, Jeremiah Wright, race now plays the role that class did in earlier Marxism.[3] In other words, the religious convictions of Barack Obama (if he shares Wright's views) has direct implications for American politics, if for no other reason than Marxism is fundamentally incompatible with the very idea of America. The convictions of Bachmann, Perry, and Santorum seem rather benign by comparison.

None of this interested Bill Keller.

I realize that complaining about media double-standards is the lowest-hanging fruit in political discourse in this country, and I promise you that this book will not dwell on it. But more troubling still is the fact that Bill Keller's essay was (even putting it charitably) childish. He appears to be incredibly ignorant of some of the most basic elements of evangelical Christian theology.

This book is partly for the Bill Kellers of the world. It is for non-Christians who, being at best marginally informed of what an evangelical theology might teach about political issues, are susceptible to the various scaremongering techniques employed by some rather paranoid progressives to foment fear among the electorate: hysterical caricatures of the "Radical Religious Right," "Christianists" (as Andrew Sullivan calls them), or "American Taliban" who are, we are told, intent on dragging America back to the Stone Ages. In the following chapters I intend to explain what an evangelical Christian theology teaches (or ought to, anyway) about the major political issues of our day. This evangelical view may or may not be popular, and might even remain unpopular by book's end. I am not so delusional as to think I will win everyone over. Nevertheless, I want progressives who fear evangelical conservatives to realize one thing: the views that are, by and large, held by evangelical Christians in America are *morally and rationally principled* views. They are not the products of racism, xenophobia, bigotry, hatred, ignorance, or anything of the sort, which is the operating assumption of far too many journalists and opinion shapers today.[4] Conservative evangelicals have solid, principled foundations in Christian theology. And I am in agreement with Peter Leithart, who writes that "Christians should be transparent about the theological sources of our political convictions," and this book is an effort at such transparency.[5]

4

I intend this as sort of a handbook for liberal journalists and public figures, in the hopes that we can move beyond caricaturing the evangelical Christian voter, candidate, or public figure as some sort of alien creature never before seen on these shores. Rather, such people embody a tradition of faith intersecting culture that has been around a millennium and a half longer than the Enlightenment secularism that so many now take for granted. That fact says something very important about the culture war in America. For hundreds of years Americans have lived with a broad moral consensus, a residue or byproduct of the explicitly Christian heritage of the English-speaking peoples. Within this consensus the typical Christian has gone about his business, and has only been (most recently) aroused to political action when that moral consensus began to be eroded by radical progressivism in the latter-half of the 20th century. The popular narrative that Christians are obsessed with abortion and contraception, homosexuality and same-sex marriage is at once mystifying and infuriating. Mystifying because it seems fairly obvious, from the Christian standpoint, at least, that the aggressors in the so-called culture war are those seeking to undermine the broad moral consensus we've enjoyed for hundreds of years. Infuriating because— well, perhaps an illustration will help. Imagine a group of squatters enters your house and demands to know why *you* are trespassing! This is an apt metaphor for how secularism has taken over the public square. Anti-Christians act like they alone are the rightful owners of America, title and deed. Somehow Christians are the trespassers, and the prospect of them being active in the public square is something frightening and illegitimate. Only complete historical amnesia or ignorance can account for this. The Western world was built by Christianity and has enjoyed prosperity and success largely because of a broadly Christian moral consensus.[6] It takes a lot of nerve for the Bill Kellers of the world to make Christianity some kind of fringe movement.[7]

But I also have another audience in mind. The conservative evangelical right is aging. Those who joined Jerry Falwell in the heady days of the Moral Majority have a lot of gray hairs to show for it. Yes, some of them might be due to Jerry Falwell himself, but most simply because of the passage of time. In my experience there is a multitude of younger evangelicals who are wary of the politics of their parents and, for a number of reasons, are abandoning conservative political principles. They are the ones selecting "Other" on their Facebook profiles.

One reason is ideological, plain and simple. The "God Is Not a Republican!" slogan is having an effect. Many have come to share the belief that somehow politics belongs to an entirely separate realm from religion and that God simply doesn't care about political issues, or they have embraced postmodern multiculturalist pragmatism and deny that one set of principles is better than any other. Yet another reason for the defection is, I suspect, psychological: being "progressive" in our day is really cool and trendy (even down to the word itself!) and many younger evangelicals (being human beings, after all) crave acceptance and desire to be relevant. Then there is, of course, the sociological element: it is simply true that youth often rebel against their parents. While smokin' in the boy's room and R-rated movies worked for fundamentalists of an older generation, wearing Obama "Hope" T-shirts is the thrill of choice for many 21st century evangelical youths. This book is for those among the evangelical ranks tempted by the alluring promises of progressivism. If I want to inform the Bill Kellers of the world, I want to *remind* evangelicals of what their faith teaches about current political matters.

And I will not keep you in suspense. I will admit and stipulate up front that God is not a Republican. That is not admitting much, because neither is he a Democrat. Like Treebeard in Tolkien's *Lord of the Rings*, he isn't on anybody's side. He's on his own side. We need to ask the right question: of all the options along the current political spectrum, whose ideology *most conforms* to God's?

This is the question this book is intended to help answer. But before we launch into an answer, there are four preliminary issues that need to be addressed.

I. THE REALITY OF REVELATION

This all assumes that God's will can be known, an idea that may be objectionable for many, if not most, readers. Remember, however, that in this book I am seeking to set forth and explain a political approach grounded in evangelical theology. And belief in God's revelation is simply in the DNA of evangelicalism. It is true that evangelicalism as a movement is a diverse, even fragmenting entity. Nevertheless, as I am using the term, it describes people *who believe that the Bible is God's self-revelation.* If I am to explain what the Bible means (or ought to mean) for evangelical politics, then I must take this for granted. And that means that if you are not in the Bible-is-God's-Word camp, you get to grant me the point purely for the sake of argument.

This is not the place to fully explain or even defend the doctrine of revelation, the formation and character of the Bible, or the claims of the gospel. My point is simply that evangelical Christian theology believes that God has spoken in the Bible. The why and how is a question for another time and place. As an evangelical theologian I am going to assume the Bible is a text that can be rightly interpreted; it has an author (God) whose communicative intent can be discerned; and we can, therefore, conform our thoughts accordingly. Again, this is not the place to defend that view, even though I realize how thoroughly passé such a literary theory is these days. But this has been the view of Christians for

2,000 years, and I remain undeterred and unimpressed by very recent (20th century) French linguistic philosophers who say otherwise. Or at least I *think* they say otherwise; quite impossible to tell, really. Since they use words, I presume all their communicative intent is immediately lost. (*What's good for the goose is good for the gander*, the saying goes!)

So the Bible will be the recurring touchstone of my presentation. I will seek to glean from it principles and foundations for politics, which I will then apply to current political issues in our context. I realize, of course, that in certain circles this belief in divine revelation is already proof-positive of ignorant fanaticism. Many are those who seek to keep public discourse religion-free. Only the secular, faith-free opinions (of the squatters) can and should be expressed in public dialogue, the thinking (or, sometimes, bullying) goes. Although this is not really the place for a thorough refutation of that opinion, I will simply point out that more than a few highly impressive thinkers with no agenda of carrying water for evangelical Christians have been quite busy putting the lie to that way of thinking.[8] The truth is that everybody has a basic standpoint that is first believed rather than proven, however much some deny it. Secular discourse likes to pride itself on only trading in "facts" and "evidence" rather than "faith" or "ideology" but, as legal theorist Steven D. Smith cogently argues, the truth is that purely "secular" discourse actually has to smuggle in all sorts of ideological artifacts into their supposedly faith-free public discourse. And if the secularists get to do it, then so do I. Except that, as a Christian, I do not believe in concealing or smuggling in my starting assumptions. So I am helpfully telling you at the outset that I am an evangelical Christian who believes the Bible and believes that the Bible applies to political issues. There! Nothing hidden, secretive, sinister, smuggled, or ulterior. I'm afraid I've just undercut the business of those websites that track the "secret" agenda of the radical Christian right. There is nothing secret about it.

2. POLITICAL THEORY AND PERFECTIONISM

So back to the question: of all the options along the current political spectrum, whose ideology most conforms to God's? The words "most conforms" are tricky ones. This seems to suggest that total or absolute conformity is not possible, and that is, in fact, what I mean. Christian theology is clear that the world as we know it is not a perfect place; far from it. In theological jargon, it is a "fallen" world. Sin has entered the world and will not be eradicated until the very end of time. This means that perfection*ism* is completely incompatible with a Christian worldview. A Christian view of civil society, then, is a sober one. It is constrained by the reality that people fall short and that perfection cannot, in the nature of the case, be achieved. As we will see in Chapter 1, this is quite different from progressivism's point of view. Progressivism, which is rooted in 19th century German philosophy (particularly G.W.F. Hegel [1770-1831]), is convinced that humanity is perfectible in history as we know it. Political programs built on this Hegelian ideal are therefore oriented toward creating the perfect, enlightened, utopian society in the here-and-now. They have what Thomas Sowell calls an "unconstrained" vision for humanity; that is, human beings are not constrained by the realities of sin or imperfection. And I cannot neglect to mention (indeed, it should be repeated as often as possible) that the track record of Hegelian political projects in utopia-building is, by any fair standard, obscene. It is at the root of two world wars, the horrific genocide of the Third Reich, and the millions of corpses (100+ million, in fact) left in the wake of 20th century communist revolutions. It is quite bemusing that for some people the most fearsome development is *Christians* in politics!

Nevertheless, progressivism rolls on, always convinced that construction of the perfect society just hasn't yet been tried by the right people.

There is an irony here, however: many conservatives are, in fact, perfectionists. They refuse to vote for a candidate that does not have each and every policy box correctly checked. They are completely unwilling to brook any compromise. For them, in order for politics to be principled, it must be an all-or-nothing affair. They are not looking to identify the "mostly conforms" but the "totally conforms." Whether they are Ron Paul supporters or the typical single issue voter, their political views have more in common with progressivism's unconstrained vision than they do with the Bible. Because the Bible teaches, quite clearly, what Sowell calls the "constrained" vision. The Bible's vision for societal well-being is not pie-in-the-sky idealism (Hegel) but incremental realism. This requires, then, wisdom and discernment, virtues repudiated by small-minded political perfectionists of all stripes, whether progressive or conservative.

3. WHAT IS AN "EVANGELICAL"?

The title of this book includes the words "Evangelical Theology." I have already mentioned, but feel the need to reiterate, that the term "evangelical" as I am using it encompasses people who believe that God reveals his will for human beings in the Bible (preeminently in the work of Jesus Christ for salvation), and that what the Bible teaches is relevant to human behavior in the here-and-now. This is purposely very broad. Not only does this wide net snag mainstream non-denominational evangelicals, but also Baptists, Pentecostals, Lutherans, Presbyterians, and many socially-minded Eastern Orthodox and Roman Catholics. Are there important differences between all these groups? Of course there are. But each of them believe (with distinctive nuances, of course) that the Bible is God's revelation to humanity. And, while my definition is broad, it still has the benefit of excluding those who retain the religiosity of Christianity while treating the Bible as a dead-letter (i.e., many in mainline Protestant churches). I do not mean this to offend, and I am certain it won't. The very last thing the mainline Episcopal church (for one example) wants is to be labeled "evangelical"! They will, no doubt, thank me for leaving them out. Furthermore, we will see throughout this book that the political liberalism rampant in mainline churches goes hand in hand with their assessment of the Bible. It should be no surprise that treating the Bible as a dead letter coincides with progressive politics. As we will see from start to finish in this book, a living Bible, one in which God speaks with authority, is incompatible with the worldview of progressivism.

The broad definition I am using has its liabilities. I have no doubt, given the distinctions between the various groups, that there will be periodic moments of disagreement among those I'm calling evangelicals. But when all is said and done, I am hopeful that the purposely broad theological perspective I offer here can be affirmed by Protestant, Roman Catholic, and Orthodox alike, even if I happen to speak from time to time in my native dialect of the Calvinist Reformation (full disclosure).

4. IS AN EVANGELICAL POLITICAL THEORY EVEN POSSIBLE?

A certain conventional wisdom is shared by many all across the political spectrum that it is impossible to derive political views from the Bible and that even the attempt is foolish. This recently became a "live issue" once again when the President of the United States addressed the National Prayer Breakfast and argued that his policies of wealth redistribution were inspired by Jesus! Specifically, Mr. Obama alleged to have gotten his idea for higher taxes on the wealthy to benefit the poor from Jesus' maxim, "to whom much is given, much is required." This was met with widespread derision, and rightly so, but often for the wrong reasons. It is oh-so-tempting to foreclose the possibility of such pontification by ignorant civil leaders by arguing that moving from the Bible to policy is misguided *as such*. And that is precisely where many pundits ended up: invoking the Bible in support of any public policy issue should be off-limits. And it is not just journalists, editorialists, and pundits who share this conviction. Even mainstream evangelical political theorists agree!

For example, in his otherwise excellent historical work, *The Contested Public Square: The Crisis of Christianity and Politics*, Greg Forster makes this sweeping claim: "All attempts to find a broader political theory in the Bible are cases of eisegesis (bringing a preferred theory to the text and interpreting the words in whatever way makes them endorse the preferred theory) rather than exegesis (allowing the text to determine our interpretation of its meaning)."[10] Really? All attempts are just reading a preferred theory into the text?

This kind of approach results in separating the Bible from public policy as two distinct, hermetically-sealed spheres, and it cannot be sustained for long. In fact, it isn't sustained for long in Forster's own book! He goes on to add in the very next paragraph: "This is not to say that the Bible provides absolutely no specifics about justice that are relevant to politics." But which is it? Either all attempts at deriving a political theory from the Bible are misguided (eisegesis), or the Bible can and does have something to say about political theory (exegesis). The incoherence is finally expressed on the following page: "The Bible forbids theft but does not, for example, endorse capitalism over socialism." The problem here is obvious: socialism is the eradication of private property. It defines theft out of existence. By forbidding theft, the Bible absolutely, at a minimum, endorses private property rights and rejects full-fledged socialism. So while taking the view that the Bible provides no political theory sounds erudite and reasonable, it is actually quite simplistic and impossible to consistently maintain.

Or consider the view of historian D. G. Hart, who writes: "[T]o try to find a biblical warrant for political positions is invariably a violation of Christian liberty. The reason is that in matters where Scripture is silent— which would include most aspects of domestic and foreign policy— Christians have liberty to act according to their consciences."[11] This really does create an impenetrable wall between Christianity and the public square. Finding biblical warrant for political positions is *invariably* a violation of Christian liberty? The area on which the Bible is silent includes *most aspects* of domestic and foreign policy?

First, notice the flagrant contradiction between his "invariably" and "most" aspects. By "most" he means there are, in fact, some political things guided by biblical principle. Therefore, by definition it is not "invariably" a violation of Christian liberty to find biblical warrant for political positions. This is a self-refuting argument. Second, that is an intentionally ambiguous "most," because it provides Hart a nifty safety-valve when his view gets uncomfortably close to its logical conclusion. Think of what it might mean: on issues like the role of government, individual property rights, whether weaker members of society are entitled to legal protection, limits (if any) to scientific research, laws governing the recognition and well-being of marriage, how to alleviate poverty, what moral principles should govern crime and punishment, or even modern warfare, Christians are completely free of guidance. We are just as in the dark as anyone else. Hart himself recognizes how radical this proposal is, which is why he uses the weasel-words "most aspects." He reserves the right to find biblical guidance on "some" issues, but for everybody else it is "invariably" wrong-headed. Thus, just as with Forster's formulation, the attempt to segregate the Bible in principle from the political issues of our day is simplistic and, as evidenced by Hart's own slippery admission, impossible to maintain. I would simply add that one of the purposes of this book is to turn Hart's position on its head: he believes the Bible is only relevant to some issues, but irrelevant to most. On the contrary, we will see that the Bible speaks to most of the pressing political issues of our day and is completely silent on a few. Hart has the ratio completely upside-down.

There are few people in the world I admire more than Pastor Tim Keller of Redeemer Presbyterian Church in New York City. His *New York Times* bestselling book, *The Reason for God*, is probably the finest popular defense of Christianity since C. S. Lewis's *Mere Christianity*. I was disappointed when, at a public forum at Columbia University, he steadfastly refused to say that Christianity has any political implications. Fearing the great danger of identifying Christianity with any particular political party or agenda, he declared: "Christianity is bigger than that." But this is exactly the inverse of reality: the more Christianity lacks specific application to real-world, public square, political problems, the smaller Christianity becomes. The more Christian doctrine simply hovers above petty political problems, the *narrower* it becomes. I appreciate Keller's situation, pastoring a burgeoning and very diverse congregation in one of the largest cities in the world. I further appreciate that he has priorities, and preaching and teaching the salvation of sinners ranks significantly higher than making declarations on politics. But his view that Christianity is bigger than politics, and therefore has nothing particular to say about political issues, is wholly artificial and accomplishes the opposite of what he thinks: a vastly smaller Christian vision.

Non-theologians feel the complexity of all this, as well. When the President justified his class war by appealing to Jesus, John Hinderaker of the influential blog *Powerline* rightly wrote: "It wouldn't be correct to say that Christianity has nothing to do with politics [...]" (showing better instincts than Hart and Keller!) and then added:

> What is unfortunate is when partisans in both church and state try to enlist Christianity, or other religious faiths, not just on matters of life and death, but on one side or another of every petty partisan controversy. Barack Obama is not alone here: my own denomination, the Evangelical Lutheran Church in America, has issued position papers on everything from banking regulation to agriculture policy—every one of which, remarkably, coincided with the position then held by the most liberal wing of the Democratic Party. The Bible offers us guidance on many topics, but as to whether the top marginal income tax rate in 21st century America should be 35% or 39%, it is silent. Although, of course, it never hurts to keep those many injunctions against covetousness in mind.[12]

I am sympathetic with much of this complaint (for reasons which will become clear as this book progresses), but again, just as with Forster, the problem appears in that last sentence: "[I]t never hurts to keep those many injunctions against covetousness in mind." Indeed! Hinderaker implicitly understands that the ethics of the Bible do, in fact, have some rather direct implications for politics and public policy.

So I remain far from persuaded by those who want to insist that the Bible and political theory are just two separate topics, two distinct universes, two parallel tracks that do not meet. As we've just seen, even those insisting on that principle are unable to be consistent with it. Moreover, I have already pointed out that many philosophers are increasingly recognizing this. For example, English philosopher Simon Critchley writes, "with no particular joy," that religion and politics are not meant to be untangled: "All political forms are best understood as sacred ideas in political dress."[13] This is not to say the issues are simple. Far from it!

But St. Paul wrote that "All Scripture is God-breathed and is useful for teaching, rebuking, correcting and training in righteousness, so that the man of God may be thoroughly equipped for every good work" (2 Tim. 3:16-17). By "thoroughly equipped" and "every good work," I take that to include the work of politicians and civic leaders.

It is true that when we get down to policy specifics (e.g., tax rates, appropriate speed limits), the Bible is often silent. But that should never obscure the fact that the Bible also provides a broad moral foundation *on which specific policies must rest.* That there is a "law above the law," or a transcendent standard to which earthly laws must conform not only has ancient classical precedent (e.g., Sophocles, *Antigone*), it is basic to the very idea of Western liberty (e.g., the *Magna Carta*, Rutherford's *Lex Rex*, the Declaration's "laws of nature and of nature's God"). It will not do, as with Forster, to pretend that the Bible's prohibition of theft means nothing for specific economic theories. Or that the Bible's teaching on the dignity of human life means nothing for the specific policy questions of abortion, embryonic stem cell research, or euthanasia. I will readily admit that the broad moral foundation does not always clearly point the way on a specific policy question. But I will equally insist that it often does. And I find that many evangelicals are very good at insisting that the "Bible is silent" on this or that issue, or "the Bible is not a handbook for [X]"; they are sometimes substantially less enthusiastic at pointing out when the Bible speaks loud and clear. In other words, when D. G. Hart is adamant that the Bible gives no guidance on "most aspects" of politics, we are always left to wonder what isn't included in that "most."

I am seeking to avoid two extremes. On the one hand, I think we ought to avoid the notion that the political sphere is insulated from the Bible as a matter of principle. This is impractical and intellectually untenable, as we have already seen. On the other hand, I think we ought to avoid what John Hinderaker notes about his denomination: the notion that the Bible speaks—and speaks clearly—to each and every policy question. Not only does this take place in liberal churches, it is becoming more frequent even in evangelical churches. A notorious example in recent years is Pastor Rick Warren of Saddleback Church in Southern California feeling compelled to speak out on the topic of anthropogenic climate change. Notice that both approaches are really trying to predetermine the relationship between the Bible and policy by appealing to a flawed principle. Call it the "all-or-nothing" principle. Either the Bible explicitly addresses everything with equal clarity (e.g., the ELCA and its policy papers) or it addresses nothing (e.g., Forster's "All attempts are eisegesis..." or Hart's "invariably"). Our two extremes just take opposite sides of the principle. In contrast to both, the question of how the Bible applies to various questions needs more than an abstract principle: it takes wisdom and discernment.

This book is designed to help with exactly that. It is arranged in three parts. These three parts correspond to three important ideas found in the Bible, and these ideas apply to three constellations of political issues in our day. And, rather helpfully, these constellations represent the proverbial "three-legged stool" of contemporary politics: social issues, economic or fiscal issues, and foreign policy issues.

The three ideas are deceptively simple. They all stem from the basic Christian confession found in 1 John 4:16: "God is love." It is God's very nature to love, and this book is arranged around three objects of his love:

God loves *people*.

God loves *prosperity*.

God loves *justice*.

Controversial stuff, I know. But I did say these are deceptively simple ideas. They may be simple, but they are simultaneously deep and profound. They have direct implications for the three great areas of political debate in America. That "God loves people" means something for moral and social issues. That "God loves prosperity" means something for economics. And that "God loves justice" means something for crime and punishment, as well as war and foreign affairs.

In the following chapters, we will explore just what, exactly, that meaning is. We will find that, according to a biblical worldview:

PART ONE (PEOPLE):

A culture must value and protect human life to flourish.

A culture must value and protect marriage and procreation to flourish.

PART TWO (PROSPERITY):

A culture must value and protect private property to flourish.

A culture must value and protect economic freedom and incentives to flourish.

PART THREE (JUSTICE):

A culture must value and protect its citizens from domestic injustice to flourish.

A culture must value and protect its citizens from foreign injustice to flourish.

---

1.   See, for example, the case of Canyon Ferry Road Baptist Church in Helena, Montana: http://caselaw.findlaw.com/us-9th-circuit/1026912.html

2. Bill Keller, "Asking Candidates Tougher Questions About Faith," The *New York Times*, August 25, 2011 (http://www.nytimes.com/2011/08/28/magazine/asking-candidates-tougher-questions-about-faith.html)

3. C.f., Anthony Bradley, *Liberating Black Theology: The Bible and the Black Experience in America* (Nashville: Crossway, 2010)

4. For a lengthy response to those stoking fear of a coming Right-Wing "theocracy," see Ross Douthat, "Theocracy, Theocracy, Theocray," *First Things* (August/September 2006) (http://www.firstthings.com/article/2007/02/theocracy-theocracy-theocracy-5

5. Peter Leithart, "Rick Santorum and Secular Natural Law," First Things, February 24, 2012 (http://www.firstthings.com/onthesquare/2012/02/rick-santorum-and-secular-natural-law)

6. C.f., Marcello Pera, *Why We Should Call Ourselves Christians: The Religious Roots of Free Societies* (Encounter Books, 2011); *Rodney Stark, The Victory of Reason: How Christianity Led to Freedom, Capitalism, and Western Success* (NY: Random House, 2006).

7. I would also add that the notion that Christians are obsessed with abortion and homosexuality is demonstrably false. David French researched the budgets of the leading "culture war" organizations (e.g., Focus on the Family) and compared them to the budgets of leading Christian anti-poverty groups (e.g., World Vision). He found that the budget of the smallest anti-poverty group examined was more than every "pro-family" organization *combined*. Evangelicals spend the vast amount of their money and effort fighting human suffering, not culture wars. See David French, "Are Christians Obsessed With Gays and Abortion?" *Patheos,* March 14, 2011 (http://www.patheos.com/Resources/Additional-Resources/Christians-Obsessed-With-Gays-and-Abortion-David-French-03-14-2011-)

8. E.g., Stanley Fish, "Are There Secular Reasons?" February 22, 2010, The *New York Times* (http://opinionator.blogs.nytimes.com/2010/02/22/are-there-secular-reasons/); Steven D. Smith, *The Disenchantment of Secular Discourse* (Cambridge: Harvard University Press, 2010); Simon Critchley, *The Faith of the Faithless: Experiments in Political Theology* (New York: Verso, 2012).

9. In this regard, I can hardly do better than recommend Jonah Goldberg, *The Tyranny of Cliches:How Liberals Cheat in the War of Ideas* (NY: Sentinel, 2012).

10. Greg Forster, *The Contested Public Square: The Crisis of Christianity and Politics* (Downers Grove: IVP Academic, 2008), 30.

11. D.G. Hart, "Bad Faith, Good Politics?" *New Horizons,* February 2012 (http://www.opc.org/nh.html?article_id=735)

12. John Hinderaker, "A Lousy President and A Lousy Theologian," *Powerline*, February 4, 2012 (http://www.powerlineblog.com/archives/2012/02/a-lousy-president-and-a-lousy-theologian.php)

13. "Tea With Simon Critchley: The Separation of Church and State Is Impossible" *The New Yorker*, February 15, 2012 (http://www.newyorker.com/online/blogs/books/2012/02/simon-critchley-faith-of-the-faithless.html)

PART ONE
PEOPLE

CHAPTER ONE

GOD LOVES PEOPLE

Evangelical theology provides a foundation for how to view the world. Or, better, it provides a basic orientation for how to interpret "Life, the Universe, and Everything" (to borrow Douglas Adams's lovely phrase from *The Hitchhiker's Guide to the Galaxy*). Particularly, what the Bible teaches about our origins, the nature of the cosmos in which we find ourselves, and our ultimate purpose or destiny provides the parameters by which we interpret the world around us. Everyone has tinted ideological lenses through which they see the world, and everything is colored accordingly. For evangelicals, the basic impulse is to have the Bible provide the lens.

In this chapter I will outline some of the parameters or "tint" that should inform an evangelical view of politics (particularly as they relate to issues of life and sexuality), and a stark contrast will emerge from one major ideological option in the modern American political scene: progressivism. In saying this I am clearly exposing myself as partisan. People with no partisanship, no axe to grind, don't bother writing books; and the fact is that everyone is partisan in some way. So I will show my hand and be as up-front as I can: *a political orientation rooted in the worldview of the Bible is irreconcilable with political progressivism*. Note well that this divide goes deeper than the Republican/Democrat partisan divide. I am talking about the more basic worldview orientation that stands behind the party divide in America. There are, I am sure, Democrats who do not buy wholesale the worldview of progressivism and there are many Republicans who do embrace progressive tendencies (e.g., powerful managerial state). However, these are exceptions. It cannot be denied that the political liberalism in America embodied in the Democrat party is closely aligned with the worldview of progressivism. In the 1960s the Democrat Party enthusiastically threw in with a progressive radicalism that drew deeply from the well of European postmodern philosophy.

So often political pundits and journalists speak of the political divide in America as if it were the difference between vanilla and chocolate. Every divide is due to, we are told, "petty partisan differences" (with emphasis on the *petty*) which we are lectured to lay aside. This kind of rhetoric gives the impression that political visions are not coherent sets of principles, but giant bundles of discrete policy preferences that can be accepted or disregarded on mere whim. "I'm fiscally conservative, but socially liberal," people often say. This assumes that there is nothing that unites liberal or conservative views of money and morals, no coherent worldview that binds the two together. But political issues are not a cluster of individual trees; they are a forest full of interlocking, networked roots. The partisan divide is not simply one of "petty partisan differences" (although it can be); it is more often a collision of entire worldviews.

THE "UNCONSTRAINED" VISION

In the introduction I briefly called attention to economist Thomas Sowell's classic book, *A Conflict of Visions*.[1] Sowell cogently draws a fundamental distinction between a politically conservative outlook and a politically liberal or progressive outlook using the terms "constrained" and "unconstrained." This is his helpful attempt to get at the bigger picture, seeing the whole interlocking forest instead of just individual trees. Rather than focusing on specific policy differences between left and right, Sowell examines the prior-held basic beliefs (competing visions) that result in specific policy preferences. Why is it that on political issues that appear to have nothing to do with each other we find the exact same people lining up on opposite sides? Sowell ingeniously recognizes that this cannot be sheer coincidence, nor can it be a self-conscious conspiracy. To understand this takes getting at the background beliefs that result in coherent political philosophies. If we don't reflect on our own background "vision," our overall worldview, we end up picking and choosing policy preferences like different flavors of ice cream; that is, arbitrarily. But, recognizing that Sowell's terms are fairly abstract and difficult to understand, allow me to explain.

An unconstrained vision is one in which human potential is not fundamentally hindered by anything. Humanity does not have any inherent obstacles. There is nothing stopping human beings from developing to their full potential or even the whole of human society achieving perfect peace and prosperity. Utopia, the world of perfect equity and justice, is within our grasp; with just a little hard work and elbow grease, a necessary amount of force, and/or a lot of education, we can overcome the evils of ignorance, hatred, and bigotry. This unconstrained vision of progressivism, writes Jay Cost, is the "public-spirited governing philosophy" of the American left. "This is the ideology that animates the pages of *The New Republic, The Nation*, and well-intentioned liberals everywhere: The idea that a powerful central government can bring about social justice and true equality."[2] Indeed, given the evolutionary worldview undergirding this vision, human progress is not only unhindered and unconstrained, but also inevitable. This kind of vision was perfectly captured for our generation in John Lennon's famous song "Imagine," which extols the advent of a world without heaven or hell, no borders or boundaries, no religion, no conflict, no possessions, a universal "brotherhood of man" in which the "world will live as one." In the unconstrained vision, nothing in nature itself can ultimately hinder human potential and progress. The cosmos is a place of absolute possibility. Anything is possible, even establishing heaven on earth. As Lennon (and *Lenin*) might say: "It's easy if you try."

As it relates to political philosophy, while having a lengthy historical pedigree, this unconstrained vision has been most recently grounded in the evolutionary worldview of highly influential German philosopher G.W.F. Hegel, whose vision of the end of history was very much the same as John Lennon's: heaven is not in the hereafter, but in the *here-and-now*. Hegel's philosophy later provided the architecture for the political vision of Karl Marx.

More important to know is that for Hegel and his successors the primary engine by which this utopia would be achieved is an all-powerful, totalitarian State. And I do not mean "totalitarian" necessarily as a bad word. It simply means a State interested in the totality of life, a State that does not turn a blind eye to any area of life where there is human suffering, a State that lets nothing fall through the cracks, a State that produces equity wherever inequity exists. The State is fundamentally benevolent, in Hegel's mind, for it has humanity's best interests at heart. It is through the power of an all-encompassing, benevolent State that humanity will overcome that which entangles and hinders human progress (e.g., "petty partisan differences," racial and social conflict, economic inequalities). After all, if people are going to relinquish their pride and prejudices (not to mention their property), someone is going to have to make them. What better institution than the one with inherently coercive power: civil government?

If all this seems like a tall order, that is because it is. One of Hegel's most famous quotes is that "[T]he State is the march of God through the world." You want divine incarnation? You want God to reveal himself? Don't go looking for a manger in Bethlehem. Look to the benevolent, almighty State. It is He, not the God of Abraham, Isaac, Jacob, who "works all things for good." The State is, for all intents and purposes, God. And that explains why, when referring to progressivism's view of the State, I am capitalizing it. For its claims are nothing less than the claims of Deity. Do I exaggerate? I seem to recall a certain Presidential candidate in 2008 promising to make the oceans recede. Yes, that was ridiculous campaign hyperbole; but very revealing hyperbole, nonetheless.

Never mind two world wars. Never mind the Holocaust. Never mind Fascism. Never mind the Communist revolutions. These were simply imperfect attempts at building Hegel's unconstrained utopia with some (perhaps) unfortunate collateral damage. Notwithstanding the unspeakable human suffering this unconstrained vision unleashed on the world, the basic, underlying idea is amazingly still embraced by political progressivism today. It is the rationale behind why, for liberal progressives, there is no realm in our entire civic order beyond government reach. No area of life where a government program or regulation is not just what the doctor ordered. No inequality can be tolerated or left alone to work itself out (i.e., markets cannot be free). Just as human nature is unconstrained, so also the State. In 1908 a great Dutch theologian, Herman Bavinck, came to America to speak at Princeton Theological Seminary. Coming from Europe, he was highly in tune with German philosophy at the time and was concerned about its export to America. He warned that the unconstrained vision of Hegelianism entails "magic formulas by which men make the world to be and to become in the past, present, and future everything they please. But reality scoffs at these fantasies."[3] Surveying what those magic formulas produced in the subsequent century, we can say confidently that he was right. Reality did scoff at the fantasies of a coming utopia. Andrew Sandlin rightly observes, "All statist utopias end in dystopias. Every attempt to create heaven on earth in the end creates a living hell."[4]

THE "CONSTRAINED VISION"

Christian theology provides an antithesis to the unconstrained vision, for two reasons. First, the universe is not pure possibility, whatever we might wish it to be, or uninterrupted evolutionary progress. Our "magic formulas" are exactly that: no more than David Copperfield's latest vanishing act. It sure looks good, but it is an illusion. The cosmos is constrained because, as the first article of the Apostles' Creed puts it, "God the Father Almighty" is "Maker of heaven and earth." He, not we, establishes the parameters: its origin, its nature, and its purpose. We live in an ordered universe. Second, since an event known as the "Fall" (Genesis 3), human beings are in conflict with their Maker. Rather than living in true freedom within the parameters set for them, human beings have sold themselves into bondage. Left to ourselves, apart from God's intervening grace, we are slaves to self-seeking, self-worshiping idolatry. In other words, we have a really difficult time accepting constraints of any kind. Be honest: doesn't this describe you? It certainly does me. Creation and Fall are two basic worldview-shaping ideas, and I will explore each in turn.

THE CREATED ORDER

We do not create the world; we encounter the world. The cosmos existed prior to our arrival. We do not choose our parents, our place of birth, or our early social connections. We are born into a world that is not of our making. St. Paul described this fundamental feature of reality when he once told the Greek philosophers in Athens that God, the Lord of heaven and earth, "who made the world and everything in it" also "determined the times set for them and the exact places where they should live" (Acts 17:24-26). His point is that the structure of the world and the history of the world ("times set for them") are not ours to create or control. The cosmos is "ordered." There are boundaries and laws that we cannot change; we must conform to them, not the other way around.

And this is exactly the teaching of the very first chapter of the Bible: Genesis 1. "In the beginning God created the heavens and the earth." Bam! There is the entire cosmos. The next verse says that "the earth was formless and empty." The rest of the chapter is all about shaping the earth for human habitation. He divides the cosmos into three "realms," sky, land, and sea (form), and then fills the realms with creatures that reproduce "according to their kinds."

This is not a cosmos of pure possibility or pure chance in which we might make of the world what we would like it to be. This is a God-ordained, structured reality. It displays both a magnificent unity as well as diversity (the very source from which we get our word "uni-verse"). But the universe is not simply orderly; it is ordered for a purpose. And Genesis 1 does not leave us in suspense as to what that purpose is. The cosmos was purposed for *human flourishing*.

Human beings are spectacularly special. With every other creature, God simply speaks it into existence rather matter-of-factly. But when it comes to making human beings, there is a pause. God doesn't just speak human beings into existence like everything else. Instead, he first speaks to himself. He has a consultation. He deliberates: "Let us make man in our image, in our likeness, and let them rule over the fish of the sea and the birds of the air, over the livestock, over all the earth, and over all the creatures that move along the ground" (Genesis 1:26). While God had made the birds to fill the sky, and the animals to fill the earth, and the sea creatures to fill the sea, God made human beings for an exalted purpose: to "fill the earth" and "rule" over everything! And why were they to rule? Because human beings were created in a way no other creature was: *in the image and likeness of God himself*. Human beings were created to be God-reflectors, representing him and ruling on his behalf. So after deliberating on the matter we are told: "So God created man in his own image, in the image of God he created him; male and female he created them."

Men and women are specially created. Since it is common to assume that conservative evangelical theology is somehow oppressive to women, I will note here that it is incredibly significant and unique that this ancient text incorporates both male and female into its creation account and bestows on them equal dignity as being the divine image. The Bible, far from being a source of oppression for women, accords them a dignity equaled by no other ancient literature.

Genesis 2 gives us a close-up view of the creation of humanity. God made Adam by forming him from the "dust of the ground" and then breathing into his nostrils the "breath of life." What an amazing picture! Human beings are united to the rest of creation (dust) but also transcend it (breath of life). Isn't this obviously true? We have so much in common with other animate creatures, yet in other ways we are a class of our own. We devote ourselves to self-reflection and rational thought (Truth);

we reflect on how we ought to live (Goodness); and we make aesthetic judgments (Beauty). Animals do none of these things. I know that Christians are supposed to be unsophisticated, but is it too much to point out that the secular scientific world is busy seeking to explain exactly this problem: What makes a man different from a mouse? And so far, despite cracking the genome and mapping the brain, they are absolutely stumped?[5] Normally people with plausible answers to difficult questions are not derided as stupid, but, alas, it is just so in this strange chapter in human history. At any rate, it is no wonder that the ancients marveled at what a magnificent creature is the human being! We are the unity of heaven and earth, body and soul, of the material and spiritual worlds, akin to creation but also akin to God! In an imaginative and entertaining way C. S. Lewis's character, the arch-demon Screwtape, tells his Nephew Wormwood that "Humans are amphibians—half spirit and half animal," and adds, "The Enemy's [God] determination to produce such a revolting hybrid was one of the things that determined Our Father [The Devil] to withdraw his support from Him."[6]

Because the Creator who made us in his own image is a personal God, we are persons. We are self-conscious beings; we can relate to God and to others in ways that other creatures cannot. We are "God-reflectors" in our whole being, body and soul, intellect, will, and emotions. We do not just "have" the image of God. We do not just "carry" the image of God, as though it is some kind of commodity. We are the image of God. We are the commodity. As God-reflectors, we are precious commodities. Often sociologists and economists speak of a given culture's "human capital." I will admit that is a rather uninspiring way of speaking about people, but it still hits on an important truth: human beings have unique value.

All of this means that an evangelical political theory rests firmly on the notion of *human exceptionalism*. Human beings are exceptional. God loves people more than he loves anything else in his whole creation. "What is man that you are mindful of him, the son of man that you care for him? You made him a little lower than the heavenly beings and crowned him with glory and honor" (Psalm 8:4-5). Jesus says: "Look at the birds of the air; they do not sow or reap or store away in barns, and yet your heavenly Father feeds them. Are you not much more valuable than they?" (Matthew 6:26). People have an intrinsic dignity and worth. That word "intrinsic" is crucial. It means that people do not gain dignity and worth by adding something (e.g., wealth, social status, economic productivity, etc.); they already have dignity and worth simply by existing. God creates people in his own image and likeness, he ordered the world for the benefit of people, and therefore *God loves people*. In Proverbs 8:27-31 a personification of "Wisdom" (understood in Christian theology as the pre-incarnate Son of God) says this:

> I was there when he set the heavens in place, when he marked out the horizon on the face of the deep, when he established the clouds above and fixed securely the fountains of the deep, when he gave the sea its boundary so the waters would not overstep his command, and when he marked out the foundations of the earth. Then I was the craftsman at his side. I was filled with delight day after day, rejoicing always in his presence, rejoicing in his whole world and *delighting in mankind*.

That is how God felt in creating humanity: delight. If there is any remaining doubt about the dignity involved in being human or that people are an object of God's love, simply consider this: *God himself became a human being in space and time to restore human beings to himself*. "The Word became flesh and made his dwelling among us" (John 1:14).

That settles the matter. God loves people. This simple affirmation provides a solid foundation for how Christians should think about the political issues pertaining to human life.

So reality is not a chaos in which we create meaning and order for ourselves; it is already an ordered cosmos. Reality is what reality is, regardless of whether we like it or not. We express this every time we tell somebody, "Get your head out of the sand," or "Wake up to cold, hard reality"! We know that indulging fantasies or creating magic formulas about what we wish were the case is counter-productive. God did not consult with us on the design plans of the universe. Genesis tells us that God took Adam and Eve and "placed" them in the Garden of Eden. We, too, are placed. They did not create the Garden, but they were commissioned to tend it. We did not create the world, but we are commissioned to tend it. God has set the rules and boundaries and purposes, and the Bible teaches that those rules and boundaries and purposes are supremely for the benefit and flourishing of the human race: "God blessed them and said to them, 'Be fruitful and multiply; fill the earth and subdue it'" (Genesis 1:28). Far from a constraint, these boundaries provide the scope and parameters for development and flourishing.

That is a pretty picture, isn't it? Let us now ruin it with our second great constraint.

THE FALL OF HUMANITY

We don't like God one bit and we certainly no longer appreciate his rules and boundaries and purposes. This is known in theological jargon as the "Fall." The Fall was humanity's rejection of God's ordering: Adam and Eve were to rule over the creatures, but Eve is deceived by the lowliest creature, a serpent, while Adam passively and cowardly stands by ("She gave some to her husband, who was with her..." - Genesis 3:6). God had created Adam and Eve as his image and likeness, yet now they want more: they do not want to receive moral instruction, they want to determine and experience things for themselves on their own terms (expressed in the phrase, "being like God, knowing good and evil").

The Fall was humanity's rejection of God's purposes for human flourishing. It was a rejection of the design. Knowing full well that disobedience meant curse and death, standing at the fork in the road, one path leading to life and the other to certain death, they chose death. This was, as you might imagine, the express opposite of being fruitful and multiplying. The Bible teaches that this is the root of all human dysfunction. Sin had "entered the world," the Apostle Paul says, and with it came condemnation and death to the entire human race (Romans 5:12-21).

This is not the place to explore the entire biblical story of the Fall and redemption, although it is important to know that that isn't the end of the story! Right now I simply want us to notice that the Fall provides another serious constraint on our vision. People are sinners. We do not naturally act in accordance with God's design. We do not naturally seek God's purposes and, therefore, we do not naturally pursue agendas leading to human flourishing. However much good we do in spite of ourselves, however much progress we make by God's grace, we cannot achieve heaven on earth. Adam and Eve had that opportunity. They were freely offered another tree in the garden: the Tree of Life. But that isn't the fruit they ate.

Even though we are the children of Adam, banished to wander "east of Eden," we still want the Tree of Life. We still want to create a world of immortality and perfection. But we want it on our terms, not God's. The Psalmist describes our collective war against God in vivid terms:

> Why do the nations conspire and the peoples plot in vain? The kings
> of the earth take their stand and the rulers gather together against

the LORD and against his Anointed One. 'Let us break their chains,' they say, 'and throw off their fetters' (Psalm 2:1-2).

"Chains" and "Fetters." That is how we, left to ourselves, see God's order and purpose. And so we rebel against his order and his purpose. We pretend that the world is not really the way God made it. We act as though God's design can be re-written, as if it were not a matter of built-in hardware, but simply software that we can hack into and re-imagine. We create magic formulas and make our own virtual reality where the Fall never happened, we are not corrupted, utopia is do-able, and God doesn't exist anyway! Remember the title of John Lennon's song? *Imagine*. The trouble is that sooner or later reality will, as Bavinck put it, "scoff at these fantasies." After watching *The Matrix* a delusional person might think the world is virtual reality and try, like Neo, jumping off a building. The illusion of flying will be fleeting. The results are perfectly predictable.

Now, the question might occur to you: if God intended for human beings to be fruitful and multiply and to rule over and subdue the earth, did those purposes disappear when humanity rejected him? Did the standards disappear? Was the order of things completely destroyed? Did the Fall alter God's original plans? The answer is: No! We know this because in the story God did not simply tear up the blueprints. Instead of telling Adam and Eve that they would be unable to be fruitful, he told the woman: "I will greatly increase your pains in childbearing; with pain you will give birth to children" (Genesis 3:16). Instead of telling them that their labor would yield no fruit, he told Adam: "Cursed is the ground because of you; through painful toil you will eat of it all the days of your life. It will produce thorns and thistles for you, and you will eat the plants of the field. By the sweat of your brow you will eat your food" (Genesis 3:17-19). In other words, even though humanity has fallen, God in his grace still allows some measure of fruitfulness and dominion.

Only it will always be mixed with pain, thorns and thistles, and sweat. Or, as we might put it in our common parlance: human flourishing (this side of eternity), in addition to being incomplete, will be accompanied by blood, sweat, and tears. There will always be suffering and failure. But that shouldn't obscure that God also allows, in spite of ourselves, a measure of well-being and success.

CONSTRAINED V. UNCONSTRAINED POLITICS

It might appear that I am meandering here. But this is all actually foundational to political theory. The unconstrained progressive worldview was forged on the anvils of German philosophy. The father of modern American progressivism, Woodrow Wilson, was a dedicated Hegelian. And basic to 19th century German philosophy was the notion (itself borrowed from the French Revolution) that "God is dead." By that, philosophers like Friedrich Nietzsche meant that humanity needs to dispense with the "old God," the one who was "Maker of heaven and earth." We must see ourselves as making reality as we imagine it to be rather than bowing to the constraints of a Creator. Humanity, according to Nietzsche, is capable of "killing God" and, when we do, the "Superman" will arise. We will no longer be children, taking orders from God; we will become as gods ourselves. This is why, for Hegel, collective humanity, embodied in the Almighty State, is "God walking on earth." It represents a humanity orphaned by the death of the old, dictatorial, aloof, ruthless, vengeful Deity of the Bible (as they describe him), and is maturing and auditioning to take his place. The State is the embodiment of a *divine humanity*.

In other words, seen from a theological perspective unconstrained progressivism is essentially a *continuation of the original Fall itself*. Human beings want to throw off the shackles, the chains and fetters by which we perceived ourselves bound. The delusion, as it was for Adam and Eve, is that this will lead to liberty, prosperity, human flourishing, and utopia. As history amply demonstrates, it actually leads to the opposite.

The great 20th century political scientist, Eric Voegelin, responded to this vision in a 1959 lecture in Munich, Germany.[7] He wrote that the so-called "death of God" does not bring about Nietzsche's "Superman." It does not lead to human beings rising above their dysfunctions and flourishing, but rather to human destruction. As a purely historical point, he wrote that "the murder of God is not followed by the superman, but by the murder of man." Or, provocatively: deicide is followed by homicide. Voegelin went on to describe exactly how this happened in the 20th century with its "mass ideological movements" of Marxism, Nazism, Fascism, and Communism. It is inescapable that killing off the Christian God means, simultaneously, killing off the Christian view of human beings. As we have just seen, Christianity views human beings as intrinsically dignified and valuable as being the image and likeness of God. But in the essentially godless view of progressivism, human beings are disposable if it serves the purpose of "progress." When people get in the way of utopia, when they continue to cling to the old order of thinking, when they refuse to get with the program, when they stubbornly cling to their pride and prejudices, or "their guns and their religion" (as a more recent proponent put it), their lives can become, alarmingly, quite negotiable to the revolutionaries.

It should not be doubted by any marginally informed person that this is precisely what led to the staggering bloodshed of the 20th century. What is baffling and depressing is that so many continue to embrace a worldview that ends in homicide and misery instead of life and prosperity. These days in our country it certainly disguises itself in a kinder, gentler version. That is understandable, given the track record.

The iron-fist of the coercive State has been gloved in soft, crushed velvet. We are not being forcibly coerced into being dependent cogs in the vast collective wheel of the State; we are being coddled and nurtured into it. The present-day view is, as Jonah Goldberg points out, "smiley-face fascism."[8] But a painted-on smiley face didn't make The Joker in *The Dark Knight* any less sinister.

Now, in writing this way I am not accusing any particular person of being "homicidal" and "sinister," much less comparing them to Heath Ledger's legendary Joker! Individual people are usually more complicated than ideological categories, and they may occupy rather benign places on the political spectrum. But that should not avert our eyes from the fact that there have been many full-fledged "Joker" figures in the history of progressive thought. Robespierre, Lenin, Stalin, Mao, Hitler, Mussolini, Pol Pot, and Che Guevara come to mind. And it is certainly worth exploring why their political programs produced such homicidal results. And the answer is not misapplication of political ideals, misevaluation of the readiness of human beings for progress, or that the wrong people have been in charge of implementation. As strange as it might sound in our day and age, the answer is found in theology. If one wants to kill God, one will inevitably want to finish the job by killing those who are literally the embodied reminder of him: "God-reflectors," people created in his image and likeness. People must be forcibly redefined and reshaped, as, for example, Karl Marx attempted with his new "Socialist Man." Those who refuse are simply defined out of the human race as enemies of progress. We will see this kind of thinking in action in the next chapter, since it forms the very essence of Margaret Sanger's vision for her organization, Planned Parenthood. For humanity to progress beyond its current dysfunctions, the less-desirable and unfortunate (always defined by the "experts") need to be eradicated. The ugly truth is that from its inception in the French Revolution, genocide has been in the DNA of progressivism, and there has since been an awful lot of it on the march to utopia.

Whereas Christianity teaches the inherent and inviolable dignity of human beings, progressivism is a religious replacement that subordinates individual human dignity to the cause of political progress. And "progress" is always defined as moving beyond the old, archaic ways of thinking, chief among them Christianity's concept of God and man. This was clearly the goal, for example, of the Nazis, who in their self-described Kulturkampf ("culture struggle") taught their youth to sing:

> We have no need for Christian virtue;
>
> For Adolf Hitler is our intercessor
>
> And our redeemer.
>
> No priest, no evil one
>
> Can keep us
>
> From feeling like Hitler's children.
>
> No Christ do we follow, but Horst Wessel!
>
> Away with incense and holy water pots.[9]

Creepy, isn't it? While not quite as overtly religious, so is this refrain, taught to elementary students in New Jersey in 2009:

> He said red, yellow, black or white
>
> All are equal in his sight
>
> Mmm, mmm, mmm!
>
> Barack Hussein Obama! Yes![10]

"Red, yellow, black or white" comes, of course, from a well-known Christian children's song, "Jesus Loves the Little Children": "Red and yellow, black and white / they are precious in his sight!" It is tempting to see this song as a one-off, an isolated incident of a misguided and overly-enthusiastic teacher going overboard. But, again, these things are not unrelated to or isolated from a background worldview (the replacement of "precious" with "equal" is incredibly significant). Attributing divine virtues to the State (in this case, the head of State) is and always has been a natural outflow of the progressive religion. The old way of thinking was that God cares for people through his providence; progressivism teaches that the State is the only providence. In a perverse re-writing of Phillippians 4:19, the State will "supply all your needs," from cradle to grave, according to its "riches in glory"!)

Likewise, central to the Marxist/communist worldview is atheism. Religion is, in the view of Karl Marx, the "opiate of the masses." Christianity lulls people to sleep, leaving them to languish under elite oppression by falsely promising them eternal life in the hereafter. Progressive leaders have always been clear-eyed in their conviction that if human culture is to advance, it must reject and move beyond the "shackles" provided by Christianity.

Whereas Christianity teaches that human beings flourish by adhering to God's prior ordering of the cosmos (the constrained vision), progressivism teaches that human beings flourish by rebelling against that concept of order and replacing it with any number of imaginations of what the world could be (the unconstrained vision). This is the basic divide: does the universe have a design or not? Is it hardware or software? If there is a prior design, if it is, as Christianity teaches, a matter of hardware, then human flourishing can only be achieved by *adhering to the design*. Apple's latest operating system isn't going to work on a Microsoft-based computer. Neither will human prosperity flow to a society that devalues human life.

Throughout this book we will notice a curious kind of schizophrenia in progressivism. So often have Christians been depicted as backward, ignorant, hate-filled bigots obsessed with "social" issues that it has become conventional wisdom. When evangelicals argue that progressivism does not lead to human flourishing they are derided as paranoid. When they express concern, for example, about the breakdown of the institution of the family or the social problems of widespread abortion, the progressive elite portray all this as pure crazy talk. Social problems? What social problems? Breakdown of the family? What breakdown? They do not see their magic formulas as magic. Everything is progressing just fine, thank you! And yet, on the other hand, at the same time they are worrying about, say, the problems of illegitimacy and dependency in urban areas or sounding the alarm over the fact that abortion has liquidated hundreds of millions of females from the world population (see Chapter 2). Maybe the evangelicals aren't so crazy, after all.

The magic formulas do not work. Reality scoffs at them. And when political conservatives point this out, they are jeered as "sky is falling" Chicken Littles. But no amount of jeering can change the reality. Progressive economic policies have bankrupted much of Europe, and Greece is currently on the brink of catastrophe. So the obvious thing to do, in the progressive mindset, is double-down on those policies and rack up staggering amounts of more debt! The institution of the family has experienced almost complete disintegration in the inner cities, leading to astounding levels of illegitimacy, crime, and poverty. So the obvious thing to do, in the progressive mindset, is even further undermine marriage by insisting on redefining it (making it a pure social convention). Abortion in much of the world is causing serious demographic damage by liquidating girls. So the obvious thing to do, in the progressive mindset, is defend abortion at all costs! The alleged benefits of progressivism never arrive. They cause problems, which are then addressed with...more progressivism. When heading away from the design for human flourishing causes the predictable lack of flourishing, the progressive imagination knows only one course of action: more pressure on the accelerator.

In the remainder of Part One we will view this clash of political theories as it relates to issues of human life from beginning to end (including the issues of abortion, embryonic stem-cell research, infanticide, and euthanasia) and human sexuality (the debate over the definition of marriage). And we will see that on each of these issues an evangelical politics must remain true to its basic idea: "God the Father Almighty, maker of heaven and earth," loves people and wants them to flourish by living according to their design parameters. And progressivism, on each of the topics discussed in this book, openly rejects those very designs in favor of various magic formulas. It has failed in its attempts to inaugurate utopia thus far, and it will continue to fail. Because reality, the design— again, in Bavinck's words—"scoffs at these fantasies." Or, even better, in the words of the Psalmist:

"The One enthroned in heaven laughs; the LORD scoffs at them" (Psalm 2:4)

---

1. Thomas Sowell, *A Conflict of Visions: Ideological Origins of Political Struggles* (Cambridge, MA: Basic Books, revised ed. 2007).

2. Jay Cost, "Democrats, Inc." *The Weekly Standard*, February 17, 2012 (http://www.weeklystandard.com/blogs/morning-jay-democrats-inc_629969.html)

3. Herman Bavinck, *The Philosophy of Revelation* (Eugene: Wipf & Stock, 2003), 311.

4. P. Andrew Sandlin, "Romancing Utopia" (http://www.christianculture.com/blog/blog/romancing-utopia.html)

5. James LeFanu, *Why Us? How Science Rediscovered the Mystery of Ourselves* (Vintage, 2010)

6. C. S. Lewis, *The Screwtape Letters* (NY: HarperOne, 2009), 45.

7. Eric Voegelin, *Science, Politics, & Gnosticism* (Washington: Regnery, 1968)

8. Jonah Goldberg, *Liberal Fascism: The Secret History of the American Left, From Mussolini to the Politics of Meaning* (New York: Doubleday, 2008)

9. Jonah Goldberg, *Liberal Fascism*, 365.

10. "Lyrics: Songs About President Obama," Fox News, September 24, 2009 (http://www.foxnews.com/politics/2009/09/24/lyrics-songs-president-obama/

CHAPTER TWO

ON LIFE FROM BEGINNING TO END

We saw in the previous chapter that, as their Creator, God loves people and desires their flourishing. This chapter will zoom in on the implications of this for political issues relating to human life. First, we will examine more closely what the Bible teaches about human life and its dignity and value. Then we will examine how the politics of progressivism reject this design in favor of magic formulas that result in human stagnation rather than human prosperity.

THE BIBLICAL DESIGN

One of remarkable things about the Bible is that God does not just interact with humanity on the basis of groups. He certainly does do that. For example, in the most basic sense he deals with the whole of humanity through individual representatives: Adam and Jesus Christ (Romans 5:12ff). He chose Abraham and his descendants to be his own special people (Genesis 15). Following the Exodus, he displaced the Canaanites as a whole from the land he promised to Abraham. His prophets routinely issued proclamations and judgments against entire people groups like the Assyrians and Babylonians. The Bible clearly teaches a concept of corporate solidarity where entire groups of individuals are classed together and evaluated morally.

At the same time, God deals with each and every human being on an individual level. Each human life is of ultimate interest to God! We know this because that is exactly how the Bible speaks of God's final accounting of all things, what it calls the "Day of Judgment." In the ebb and flow of human history God does deal with entire nations, raising them up or tearing them down. Yet on that final day, each and every person must give an account for themselves. In Ezekiel 18, the people of Israel were complaining, in fact, that God is unjust in dealing with the nation as a whole. Why, for example, should the children suffer because of what their parents did or did not do? God responds to this complaint by telling them that God's ultimate judgment is based on individual merits: "Every living soul belongs to me, the father as well as the son—both alike belong to me. The soul who sins is the one who will die" (Ezekiel 18:4).

Thus, the Bible teaches individual responsibility and accountability. Psalm 62:12 says, "Surely you [God] will reward each person according to what he has done." The Apostle Paul quotes this Psalm when speaking of the Day of Judgment: "God will give to each person according to what he has done" (Romans 2:6). An important principle arises from this: *individual responsibility entails individual dignity.* If each and every human being will be held to account, it means that no human being is of *no account*, worthless, or to be disregarded. If God claims that "every living soul belongs to me," and promises to deal with every single one of them, then all people are important. In other words, you have never once met an unimportant person. Our 19th century Dutch friend, Herman Bavinck, put it this way: "[E]very human person is an organic member of humanity as a whole, and at the same time, in that whole, he or she occupies an independent place of his or her own." A person is "a unique idea of God, with a significance and destiny that is eternal!"[1] More famously, C.S. Lewis:

> There are no ordinary people. You have never talked to a mere mortal. Nations, cultures, arts, civilizations—these are mortal, and their life is to ours as the life of a gnat. But it is immortals whom we joke with, work with, marry, snub and exploit—immortal horrors or everlasting splendors. This does not mean that we are to be perpetually solemn. We must play. But our merriment must be of that kind (and it is, in fact, the merriest kind) which exists between people who have, from the outset, taken each other seriously - no flippancy, no superiority, no presumption.[2]

This concept of individual human responsibility and, by extension, individual human dignity is what gave rise to the Western notion of individual rights. Individuals have an ultimate priority over their particular group. Rodney Stark explains:

> Much has been written about the origins of individualism. All of these books and articles are learned and even excessively literate, but they also are surprisingly vague and allusive, perhaps because of a reluctance to express their fundamental thesis too openly: that the Western sense of individualism was largely a Christian creation.[3]

He goes on to identify the features that led to it: "From the beginning, Christianity has taught that sin is a personal matter—that it does not inhere primarily in the group, but each individual must be concerned with her or his personal salvation."[4] Rather than being simple captives to our fate, "Christianity was founded on the doctrine that humans have been given the capacity and, hence, the responsibility to determine their own actions."[5] If this is true, it is a very short step to emphasizing human rights. Responsibility requires freedom; and when men and women are, for example, slaves, it denies them their basic right of self-determination. This led directly, as Stark documents, to the abolition of slavery in Medieval Europe.

So God does not love human life in the abstract. He loves each and every particular embodiment of his image and likeness. In the same context in which he instructs Israel that each soul will give its own account, he says: "'Do I take any pleasure in the death of the wicked?' declares the Sovereign LORD. 'Rather, am I not pleased when they turn from their ways and live?'" (Ezekiel 18:23) Note the emphasis on human flourishing: that they will turn from their ways "and live." And in this context, it clearly means that God desires that individual people will flourish by enjoying life instead of death.

Partaking of The Tree of Life was the human ideal, you will recall. Death "entered the world" with the advent of sin, and represents the exact opposite of the creation's design. Life was, and is, the very idea for the cosmos. There is a reason the Bible describes ultimate flourishing of human beings as "eternal life" (John 3:16). It is not a literary accident that the chapter immediately following the Fall of humanity in Genesis 3 records a story about murder. As if to emphasize that humanity is on the path of death rather than life, Genesis 4 tells of Cain's brutal murder of his brother, Abel. And to underscore the matter even more emphatically, Genesis 5 is a long genealogy of Adam's race. It begins with a reminder of the original design: "When God created man, he made him in the likeness of God. He created them male and female and blessed them." What follows appears to be a typical family tree, except that there is one line repeated so many times it leaps off the page: "and then he died." So and so lived, "and then he died." Eight times we are told: "and then he

POLITICS & EVANGELICAL THEOLOGY

died." People were designed for life; they were blessed and commissioned to be fruitful. But something has gone terribly wrong.

In the interest of maintaining instead of abandoning his creation, God sets about protecting human life. In Genesis 9 he reiterates the notion of individual accountability when it comes to the protection of life: "And from each man, too, I will demand an accounting for the life of his fellow man" (Genesis 9:5). And then, in what might appear an irony, he institutes the death penalty: "Whoever sheds the blood of man, by man shall his blood be shed; for in the image of God has God made man" (9:6). Far from devaluing human life, however, this command emphasizes the value of human life. Human dignity is grounded in the fact that we are image-bearers of God. The threat of death for murder positively underscores that an individual human life is of ultimate concern to God.

This is the emphasis throughout the rest of Scripture, and its most famous codification appears in the 6th Commandment: "You shall not murder." Christian theology is fundamentally, irrevocably, a life-affirming worldview. And it is not a vague, sentimental feeling, but a specific, concrete valuing of human life on the individual level. No one's life is negotiable. No one's life is of less value or importance. And that includes—especially includes—the weakest and most helpless members of society. This is illustrated very clearly in Exodus 21:22-25, which says:

> If men who are fighting hit a pregnant woman and she gives birth prematurely but there is no serious injury, the offender must be fined whatever the woman's husband demands and the court allows. But if there is serious injury, you are to take life for life, eye for eye, tooth for tooth, hand for hand, foot for foot, burn for burn, wound for wound, bruise for bruise.

There are a number of significant things about this ancient Israelite law. Leave aside for the moment the principle of retribution here ("eye for an eye"), which many people wrongly believe is an injustice. We will address that principle in Chapter Eight. First, notice that the assault is unintentional. Usually in Old Testament law unintentional manslaughter does not warrant automatic retribution; God provided what are called "cities of refuge" where someone who accidentally kills another person may flee to avoid punishment (Exodus 21:12-13). They must live out the remainder of their days in the city of refuge. But this option does not seem available in this case. Why? Because the victim is an *in utero child*. Some writers, seeking to avoid that implication, point to an ambiguity: when it says "if there is serious injury" it does not specify whether it means injury to the mother or to the child. But think about it. If the law is merely protecting the woman's injuries, then why mention that she is pregnant at all? That detail would be totally superfluous if this law only meant to protect a woman from being collateral damage in a fight! The law is intended to protect the life of mother and child. And it appears that the value placed on this unborn child is great, indeed, because it does not appear that the perpetrator could flee to a city of refuge to escape punishment! Wayne Grudem reflects on what this implies:

> This means that God established for Israel a law code *that placed a higher value on protecting the life of a pregnant woman and her preborn child than the life of anyone else in Israelite society.* Far from treating the death of a preborn child as *less significant* than the death of others in society, this law treats the death of a preborn child or its mother as *more significant* and worthy of more severe punishment.[6]

Scripture clearly teaches, then, that human life has intrinsic dignity and value. That word "intrinsic" is key. It means that human beings are valuable simply because they exist. They need no other "thing," no other attribute, no other possession, no other status in order to enjoy the right to life. That is, in fact, the only way an unborn child could have a right to life, for they literally have nothing additional to offer! And the Bible consistently grounds this individual human right to life in the fact that human beings are the "image and likeness of God." Not only is that the moral foundation for an evangelical view of right-to-life issues respecting the unborn, disabled, or elderly, it is the moral foundation for all human rights! It is true that secularism champions human rights (when convenient), but how they justify the idea is more difficult to ascertain. The truth is they borrow it from the Christian moral tradition that built the Western world and brazenly claim it exclusively as their own. They wrench the flower of human dignity from its deep, rich native theological soil and transplant it into secularist gravel. Its survival is very much in doubt.

We know it is in doubt because, as I just said, secularists champion human rights *when convenient*. For when human rights get in the way of some other perceived "good," those rights are very negotiable. It is astounding in hindsight, for example, how many intellectuals and journalists who otherwise paid lip-service to human rights deliberately looked the other way and provided cover for the Soviet Union's mass purges in the early 20th century. The Soviet Union was the model progressive utopian project, and the value of human life was sickeningly easy to subordinate to the goals of progress. Or, in the more contemporary context, consider how the inalienable right of "choice," for example, trumps the rights of a baby in the womb. The "greater good" of convenience or economic productivity sometimes trumps the rights of the disabled or elderly who are seen as a burden to society. These kinds of exceptions to the rule positively demonstrate that secularism is unable to ground its notion of human rights in anything transcendent, reliable, or stable. "Rights" are only sometimes rights, We will address this at greater length in Chapter Seven on justice.

Evangelical theology, then, is obliged to view each and every human life as intrinsically valuable and entitled to protection. That includes the life of the unborn. God clearly views the unborn as his image bearers; they are an object of delight in his eyes:

> For you created my inmost being; you knit me together in my mother's womb. I praise you because I am fearfully and wonderfully made; your works are wonderful, I know that full well. My frame was not hidden from you when I was made in the secret place. When I was woven together in the depths of the earth, your eyes saw my unformed body. All the days ordained for me were written in your book before one of them came to be. (Psalm 139:13-16)

This, coupled with the fact that elsewhere personhood is ascribed to children in the womb (Psalm 51:5; Luke 1:41-44), makes clear that unborn children are entitled to protection.

The Bible's vision for human life and flourishing, then, is grounded in the fact that we, individually, are the image and likeness of God. We are endowed with an intrinsic dignity and value by virtue of our very existence. The American Founding Fathers actually invoked this very principle: "All men are created equal and are endowed by their Creator with certain unalienable rights, among them *life*...." When it comes to the magic formulas of political progressivism, however, this theology is jettisoned and those rights seem rather, well, *alienable*.

AN ALCHEMY OF DEATH

Progressivism is, in its very nature, a collectivist vision for humanity. It subordinates the individual to the collective will. Whatever notion of greater good happens to prevail at the time takes precedence over the individual. Despite plenty of rhetoric about being humane, it very often dehumanizes the individual and subordinates him or her to the will of the majority. This has clearly been the case historically, from the French Revolution to the Communist revolutions.

In order to attempt a moral justification for this subordination, the argument always hinges (indeed, it must hinge) on defining certain people, whether they be dissidents or other kinds of enemies of the State, out of the legitimate collective. People inconvenient to progress must be made "outsiders." In Marxism, this was easily done by redefining humanity as the "Socialist Man," that is, the person who is on board with the aims of revolution. If you're not on board, then you are no longer a true human being. This is the unethical rationale of every instance of genocide in world history: this person or that group of people is not really like us. German Chancellor Kaiser Wilhelm II declared that Jews were no better than mosquitoes, and suggested that the use of poison gas was the best solution for both.[7] One of his successors, Adolf Hitler, took him all-too-seriously in the 1940s. In Rwanda in 1994, in the eyes of the Hutus the Tutsis were nothing more than "cockroaches" to be eradicated. The results were appalling.

In our culture, the redefining is a bit more subtle: a distinction is drawn between the terms *human* and *person*. The dignity and value of a human being is not a feature of simply being human; a human being needs something else to qualify for "personhood." And, as always, it is the powerful elite who get to define what that additional attribute should be. And it is an ever-changing, arbitrary standard dependent only on the immediate societal goal to be achieved. Human dignity, in other words, is not (as it is in the Bible) an intrinsic characteristic of human beings; it is an extrinsic characteristic that a human being may or may not have. Without that extra thing, whatever it may be, a person is not a legitimate participant in the collective. People become disposable. American Christians are often called "xenophobic," people who fear those perceived as the "other." Yet Christianity is a religious worldview that, at its core, doesn't believe in an "other." The only way progressivism can progress is to define as "others" those who stand in the way. In a word: it is progressivism that tends toward the xenophobic.

The euphemisms for progress and the greater good are legion: "choice," "quality of life," "productivity," "women's health," and so forth. Each of these terms is used to rationalize the eradication of a certain portion of the human race. They serve to rationalize why certain people are on the outside, not entitled to legal protection. As Voegelin both observed and predicted, the arrival of Nietzsche's Superman, humanity without a transcendent moral order, results in the systematic murder of man.

Let us examine some of the ways.

ABORTION

In 1973, when the U.S. Supreme Court handed down its landmark ruling in *Roe v. Wade*, Justice Blackmun wrote in his majority opinion that science leaves room for doubt about the status of a fetus. Is it a human being? Is it a "person," from a legal standpoint? Or is it just an inanimate lump of tissue? When does a "person" become a person? Justice Blackmun and the majority on the court professed ignorance on the matter, even though science today has soundly settled the matter: a fetus is a human being. From the moment of conception, it has its own unique DNA. The only way to keep it from developing fully is to artificially stop the process (i.e., kill it). Nevertheless, usually when one is ignorant on a matter of life and death, one "errs on the side of caution," as the saying goes. Instead, the court took the opposite route and, in effect, defined the entire class out of the legal human race, summarily sentencing some 50 million of them to execution over the following 40 years. This was all for a perceived greater good: a newly-invented Constitutional right to "privacy."

So unborn human beings were denied legal protection, subordinated to progressive standards of human sexual autonomy, aided and abetted by equally progressive interpretive strategies toward the U.S. Constitution, (i.e., it is not a document that restrains us; its meaning changes based on the current needs.) But a view of human dignity as extrinsic does not and cannot stop at the birth canal. The State granted women total sovereignty in such matters, and it appears that this sovereignty extends to exactly when the fetus becomes a child. That exact time is: whenever the mother happens to want the child. Therefore, many progressives vehemently defended the practice of "partial birth" abortion, which is as odious as it sounds. It amounts to this: *a human child is not entitled to legal protection of its life even when only a portion of its head remains in the birth canal.* At that fateful moment, a "physician" is fully justified in ramming a pair of scissors into the back of its skull and vacuuming out its brain. It bears repeating: not only does progressivism positively endorse this activity, it provides the moral and rational justification for this activity. Only widespread public outrage and shame resulted in the ban of this procedure.

INFANTICIDE

But it gets worse. In the progressive mind, *a human child is not even entitled to legal protection of its life even when it is fully born, so long as the mother's intention was abortion.* Let me restate that as clearly as I can: a child who "accidentally" survives an abortion procedure and is completely born alive is still not entitled to legal protection. It may be appropriate in that circumstance to finish the job by letting the child slowly die. If partial-birth abortion is barbaric, this is on another level altogether. It is pure infanticide, the murder of a living child. It is the rebirth of the ancient practice of "exposure," withholding care and nurture from an unwanted child, leaving it out in the cold to die. This was popular in the Roman Empire, and it was Christians that ultimately ended the practice. It is not a coincidence that as the influence of Christianity wanes in the Western world, the practice is being revived.

The biggest defender of this practice in recent American history is the current President of the United States, Barack Obama. I do not want this book to be overly partisan, but it is my moral duty to make this as public as I can, whenever I can, because far too few Americans are aware of this. The story casts Mr. Obama in such a negative light that the mainstream media outlets have provided almost unbelievable cover for him. In fact, in his final 2008 presidential debate Senator John McCain had the fortitude to challenge Mr. Obama on his support for this form of infanticide. The now-President responded with what can only be called a bald-faced lie, knowing that the compliant press would never expose it as such: "If it sounds incredible that I would vote to withhold lifesaving treatment from an infant, that's because it's not true."[8] But not only did he vote this way, he was the most outspoken spokesman for this practice on the floor of the Illinois Senate, referring to "that fetus, or child — however way you want to describe it." The facts are public record, and anyone can review them: he was advocating for withholding care to living human beings who survive a botched abortion. Andrew McCarthy comments:

> They were coming out alive. Born alive. Babies. Vulnerable human beings Obama, in his detached pomposity, might otherwise include among 'the least of my brothers.' But of course, an abortion extremist

can't very well be invoking Saint Matthew, can he? So, for Obama, the shunning of these least of our brothers and sisters — millions of them — is somehow not among America's greatest moral failings.[9]

Although it does not seem possible, it gets even worse.

Not only are unborn children not persons entitled to protection under the law, and not only are born (but unwanted) children not persons entitled to protection under the law, some progressive advocates believe that disabled children, or any child not deemed to have good prospects for a "quality" life, are not persons entitled to protection under the law! Professor of Bioethics at Princeton University, Peter Singer, is at the forefront of a progressive effort to get beyond the traditional ethics that have been at the foundation of the flourishing of the Western world. He begins his book, *Rethinking Life and Death*: "After ruling our thoughts and our decisions about life and death for nearly two thousand years, the traditional Western ethic has collapsed."[10] Singer very helpfully makes no effort to disguise the nature of his progressivism. He is the embodiment of Nietzsche's desire for humanity to "get beyond" the old, archaic, Christian view of the world. And, as I pointed out in the last chapter, this demands that the Christian view of human beings must be overcome. Right on cue, Singer says of the notions "sanctity of life," "dignity," or "image of God": "Fine phrases are the last resource for those who have run out of argument." He edited a book with the revealing title, *Unsanctifying Human Life*. In an article for the London Spectator in 1995, starkly entitled, "Killing Babies Isn't Always Wrong," he put it succinctly:

> That day had to come when Copernicus proved that the earth is not at the center of the universe. It is ridiculous to pretend that the old ethics make sense when plainly they do not. The notion that human life is sacred just because it's human is medieval.[11]

Not surprisingly, central to Singer's new ethic is a distinction between "human" and "person." Personhood is something extrinsic to existence. It is not a feature of existing, but a feature of *conscious* existing. There is the "extra." An "unconscious" human fetus, therefore, is not a person, but a "conscious" animal is a person! But that is not all. Even fully born and alive children are not persons, based on these criteria:

> Human babies are not born self-aware or capable of grasping their lives over time. They are not persons. Hence their lives would seem to be no more worthy of protection than the life of a fetus.[12]

Singer's logic leads in all kinds of directions, from euthanizing of children not deemed to have prospects for a quality life, to the euthanizing of the disabled, elderly, or anyone else not living a "productive" life. It also leads to Singer's complete denial of human exceptionalism and a radical view of animal rights. Believing that human beings are more valuable than animals is, according to Singer, "speciesism," something on a par with racism. Here we see clearly that making the first move of rejecting the Christian, Western, or, as he condescendingly calls it, "Medieval" view of humanity, and insisting that value and dignity is extrinsic to human existence leads to the *dehumanization* of anyone deemed by the powerful to be inconvenient.

Perhaps one might like to think that Peter Singer is on the outward fringe of progressivism (a difficult thing to believe of the Professor of Bioethics at Princeton University who publishes books with Oxford University Press), but he is far from alone. The Netherlands has an official policy called the "Groningen Protocol," published in the *New England Journal of Medicine*, which helps doctors to determine whether to euthanize sick or disabled children.[13] According to *The Lancet*, 8% of infants who die in Holland do so at the hands of their physicians.[14] Just earlier this year (2012) the *Journal of Medical Ethics* published a paper entitled, "After

Birth Abortion: Why Should the Baby Live?" The authors argue that the baby born alive has no more right to live than the baby in the womb, and that infanticide should be allowed regardless of the health of the child. This is from the abstract of the paper:

> Abortion is largely accepted even for reasons that do not have anything to do with the fetus' health. By showing that (1) both fetuses and newborns do not have the same moral status as actual persons, (2) the fact that both are potential persons is morally irrelevant and (3) adoption is not always in the best interest of actual people, the authors argue that what we call 'after-birth abortion' (killing a newborn) should be permissible in all the cases where abortion is, including cases where the newborn is not disabled.[15]

Wesley J. Smith wisely encourages us not to let the shock of this position obscure the bigger picture, and in identifying that picture he hits the nail squarely on the head:

> 'After-Birth Abortion' is merely the latest example of bioethical argument wielded as the sharp point of the spear in an all-out philosophical war waged among the intelligentsia *against Judeo/ Christian morality based in human exceptionalism and adherence to universal human rights*. In place of intrinsic human dignity as the foundation for our culture and laws, advocates of the new bioethical order want moral value to be measured individual-by-individual — whether animal or human — and moment-by-moment. Under this view, we each must *earn full moral status by currently possessing capacities sufficient to be deemed a 'person.'* As the authors of 'After-Birth Abortion' put it, 'We take "person" to mean an individual [not just a human] who is capable of attributing to her own existence some (at least) basic value such that being deprived of this existence represents a loss to her.' In other words, if you can't value your own life, your life has less value.[16]

59

The "progression" of the logic of progressivism makes obvious that once a culture severs its moorings in the Christian moral consensus by making personhood something other than being human, the demons released from Pandora's Box cannot be rounded up, domesticated, and put back in the box. Even some people who do not travel all the way down the roads suggested by Singer and others, and who appear perfectly reasonable and willing to rethink their views on abortion, are stymied by accepting the basic premises that lead to their kind of barbarism. For example, Will Wilkinson, blogging for *The Economist:*

> I favour legal abortion. I don't think embryos or fetuses are persons, and I don't think it's wrong to kill them. I also don't think infants are persons, but I do think laws that prohibit infanticide are wise. Birth is a metaphysically arbitrary line, but it's a supremely salient socio-psychological one.[7]

While it might be nice that Wilkinson psychologically prefers living in a culture that doesn't routinely kill babies, by adopting the premise that humanness and personhood are two different things he is, in fact, left intellectually helpless to oppose just such societies. He can tell them it isn't wise all day long. That will not be very helpful or broadly persuasive when the issue is not whether babies are persons, but rather whether Jews are "mosquitoes" or Tutsis are "cockroaches." After all, why isn't having a brain, ten fingers and ten toes just as "metaphysically arbitrary" as birth?

If any of this is a shock, it shouldn't be. Political progressivism believes in a coming utopia, a world where humanity is perfected. It therefore requires efforts to biologically perfect humanity. One of the ways this has been pursued in America is through the practice of abortion, (the most influential champion of which was Margaret Sanger, founder of Planned Parenthood. The core purpose of that now-Federally funded organization was, and I quote, "to stop the multiplication of the unfit."[18] Sanger told Mike Wallace in 1957:

> I think the greatest sin in the world is bringing children into the world--that have disease from their parents, that have no chance in the world to be a human being practically. Delinquents, prisoners, all sorts of things just marked when they're born. That to me is the greatest sin—that people can—can commit.[19]

Stare at those chilling words again. "Children [...] that have no chance in the world to be a human being practically." Who, pray tell, makes that determination? Progressivism's rejection of intrinsic human dignity results in the powerful preying on the weak every time.

EMBRYONIC STEM CELL RESEARCH

The Pandora's Box extends to scientific research, as well. Lacking any ethical rationale for why a human embryo should be entitled to any more respect than bacteria growing in a petri dish, many scientists, almost always aligned with political progressivism, advocate experimenting on human embryos. The alluring promise is that human embryos are a source of pluripotent stem cells: cells that can be turned into any kind of human tissue. Pluripotent stem cells are the source of many therapies, and might provide a cure all manner of diseases.

Many do not find it troubling at all to create and then carve up human embryos precisely because they do not believe those embryos to be persons. But again: once an egg is fertilized, it becomes an entirely unique human being, complete with its own set of DNA. In the proper conditions, this "blastocyst" (impersonal terms are part of the moral insulation) will inevitably develop to maturity. The only way to stop this biological process is to... well, artificially stop it. That is, stop it before it gets to some nebulous point at which it is a person. The very fact that the process of development must be halted (usually by freezing the embryo) is proof-positive of what, exactly, we are dealing with: human beings. There is no scientific doubt about this whatsoever. (The two delightful, vibrant young girls I know who were adopted from a freezer and carried to term put an end to all doubt.) The only option available to the scientist who does not wish to be viewed as "inhumane" is to make the argument, once again, that human does not mean person. Personhood requires something else, something extra, and that "extra" is ever-changing and flexible, depending on whose interests are being advanced. As I pointed out earlier, this core ethical mistake is at the root of every genocide ever committed. The victims are not persons. They are "other."

The truth is that there are other ways of creating pluripotent cells that do not require the destruction of embryos. Umbilical cord blood, for example, is a source of stem cells and has an impressive track record of successful therapies. More recently, scientists have discovered a way to create pluripotent stem cells from normal human skin. Neither of these raises any moral or ethical questions, yet many still clamor for the Federal government to fund embryonic stem cell research. Leaving aside for the moment why the Federal government should be funding such research in the first place, the bigger question is why we should be pursuing stem cells by destroying human embryos when it is not only redundant, but morally problematic?

Many discussions of stem cell research focus on the scientific benefits and successes of either embryonic or other methods. This is irrelevant to my purpose here. I am arguing that in an evangelical Christian worldview human dignity (or to use the operative word, personhood) is intrinsic to human existence, and no amount of utilitarian successes can justify destroying what is, by all accounts, human life.

EUTHANASIA

If the alchemy of death begins with embryos, it extends all the way to the other end of the spectrum of life. Having lost the biblical moorings of human dignity, it is natural for progressives to turn their attention to another class of human beings to question their personhood.

Euthanasia is not as much of a hot-button political issue as it once was in the American context, although it occasionally flares up in the public consciousness (e.g., the Terri Schiavo case). By way of contrast, it is very much a live issue in Europe, especially Holland, where it has become so common many older citizens find it necessary to carry around cards that read: "Please, Doctor, don't kill me!"[20] Twenty-five percent of Dutch physician-assisted suicides are even without the patient's consent.[21] Holland is so cutting-edge that they have now implemented mobile euthanasia units designed to literally bring death to your doorstep.[22]

The very word, "euthanasia," indicates that it is an anti-Christian idea at its very core. It comes from two Greek words meaning "good death." If ever there were an oxymoron from the standpoint of a Christian worldview, this one surely qualifies. Christianity is an irrevocably life-affirming worldview. Death is not the design. Death is not, never has been, and never will be something good. The Apostle Paul teaches that death is fundamentally anti-creational, the very thing that God is overcoming in his work of redemption: "The last enemy to be destroyed is death" (1 Corinthians 15:26).

Euthanasia may not seem as controversial as, say, abortion and infanticide, because it brings to mind the relief of suffering. The euthanasia movement self-consciously tailors its language to invoke a noble concept: death with *dignity*. But the movement is much more than simply relieving pain and suffering as a person dies. Euthanasia is not fundamentally about palliative care. As a movement, it is purely a creature of modern progressivism. Ian Dowbiggin writes:

> Before World War I the overwhelming consensus among Americans was that physicians were justified in trying to provide their dying patients with a [sic] 'easy death' by making them as comfortable and pain-free as possible, but there was almost no public support for legalizing active mercy killing. Only when the popularity of social Darwinism, scientific naturalism, eugenics, positivism, and the ideology of Progressivism mounted at the beginning of the twentieth century, undermining faith in traditional religious beliefs, did a debate begin over whether or not the state should permit painless killing of incurable patients.[23]

Immersed in that truly toxic ideological brew, leaders of the euthanasia movement were interested in the practice as a tool of social control. It is simply a logical expansion of Margaret Sanger's desire to keep the "unfit" from reproducing. Wesley Smith observes that once the progressive attitudes toward eugenics took root, it did not take long

> to spread beyond deciding who should not be born to the presumption that society could decide who among the living should die. For many believers in eugenics, killing was not just seen as a rational means of ending suffering when life was no longer worth living because of pain or despair, but also had the potential to be an effective method of social control. Thus, in 1900, one of the euthanasia movement's pioneers, physician William Duncan McKim, advocated a 'gentle, painless death' as the solution to problems he saw caused by America's drunkards, criminals, and people with disabilities.[24]

It is helpful to return and reflect for a moment on Thomas Sowell's *Conflict of Visions*. He was trying to determine why, on issues that seem unrelated, the same people, the "usual suspects," always line up on opposite sides? The answer is that the issues are not as unrelated as it appears. There are deeper background worldviews or visions that tie the issues together. And the thread that ties together the abortion industry and euthanasia movement is their common heritage in the eugenics of early 20th century progressivism.[25] If utopia is to arrive, it needs a populace "fit" for it. Those who are "unfit" are redefined as non-persons and are therefore disposable.

REALITY SCOFFS

If the illusions are really illusions, if the magic formulas designed to biologically perfect the human race by getting rid of the unwanted and unfit are really just magic, then it stands to reason that reality will eventually intervene. If, as evangelical Christians are convinced, the very cosmos was designed for human life and flourishing, yet progressivism has relentlessly pursued its own forms of flourishing that devalue human life, then there must be significant social consequences. In what ways has reality scoffed at the fantasies?

> One might point to any number of eye-opening statistics to demonstrate the social consequences of an abortion-on-demand culture. For example, look at these abortion statistics for New York City in 2010:

Of the 208,541 pregnancies in New York City in 2010, 83,750 were terminated by abortion: 4 in 10. Among non-Hispanic blacks, there were 38,574 abortions and 26,635 live births: thus for every 1,000 African-American babies born, 1,448 were aborted. Those numbers were even more chilling among non-Hispanic black teenagers: for every 1,000 African-American babies born to teenagers, 2,630 were aborted. The overall teenage abortion rate was 63 percent in a city where 16 percent of all pregnancies were teen pregnancies.[26]

Those are appalling numbers. Not only are they the result of substantial cultural breakdown of marriage and family, a society that aborts 40% of its children cannot but cause ripple effects in all kinds of unanticipated ways. Many hardline progressives are undisturbed by those numbers, however. They may publicly lament them in the same way President Bill Clinton publicly lamented abortion, claiming to want to make it "safe, legal, and rare." But, like Clinton, they will not countenance the slightest restriction on abortion. It is worth remembering that Clinton himself vetoed the ban on partial-birth abortion not just once, but twice. Actions speak louder than words.

But reality does have a way of catching up to magic formulas and fantasies. In her groundbreaking book, *Unnatural Selection: Choosing Boys Over Girls and the Consequences of a World Full of Men*, Mara Hvistendahl, herself a firm believer and continued defender of the right to abortion, discovers some grim, unintended consequences.[27] Abortion-on-demand has created a global demographic crisis. The natural ratio of boys to girls (this is a biological law) is 105 boys to every 100 girls. If the numbers skew outside that range, something artificial or unnatural is causing it. Ms. Hvistendahl discovered, by her own accounting, that there are 163,000,000 - *one hundred sixty-three million!* - missing females in the world today, largely in Asian countries. Abortion technology has made the widespread cultural practice of selecting the desired sex of a child so easy that it has created a world literally without enough women. The irony could not be more thick; the very thing that promised to liberate women, complete reproductive autonomy and "control of their bodies," has been the instrument of the systematic eradication of women.

Hvistendahl is very worried about this because a culture with too many men and too few women "are not nice places to live." Historically speaking, there is a connection between extreme gender imbalance and violence (there is a reason it was called the "Wild" West). Where men vastly outnumber women, violence and crime are not far behind. Moreover, since the value of women vastly increases, they become at heightened risk for exploitation. And when women are at a premium and, in fact, imported from elsewhere, prostitution and the sex-slave trade results.

In Jonathan Last's *Wall Street Journal* review of Hvistendahl's book, he closes with these sobering observations:

> Despite the author's intentions, 'Unnatural Selection' might be one of the most consequential books ever written in the campaign against abortion. It is aimed, like a heat-seeking missile, against the entire intellectual framework of 'choice.' For if 'choice' is the moral imperative guiding abortion, then there is no way to take a stand against 'gendercide.' Aborting a baby because she is a girl is no different from aborting a baby because she has Down syndrome or because the mother's 'mental health' requires it. Choice is choice. One Indian abortionist tells Ms. Hvistendahl: 'I have patients who come and say 'I want to abort because if this baby is born it will be a Gemini, but I want a Libra.'
>
> This is where choice leads. This is where choice has already led. Ms. Hvistendahl may wish the matter otherwise, but there are only two alternatives: Restrict abortion or accept the slaughter of millions of baby girls and the calamities that are likely to come with it.[28]

CONCLUSION

Progressivism rejects the Christian design. Rather than having a high and noble view of humanity as the "image and likeness of God," it views its dignity as conferred by arbitrary, extrinsic factors: whether one is "fit," "productive," "wanted," "conscious," or anything else one can imagine. The result is widespread dehumanization. From an evangelical Christian perspective, this is unsurprising. Treating the hardware design for human flourishing as merely social and cultural software to be manipulated results in a failure to flourish.

This worldview divide has stark political consequences. The question I raised in the introduction should now be raised: when it comes to defending and protecting human life as inherently valuable and dignified, which agenda among the current options most conforms to God's? This is not a close call. One of the major political parties, at least in word if not deed, actively promotes a culture of life. The other party, in word and deed, actively devalues human life on the broad spectrum of issues addressed in this chapter. It is a blessed and helpful thing to have the contrast so absolute. It ought to make the task of the evangelical voter very easy.

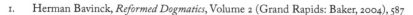

1. Herman Bavinck, *Reformed Dogmatics*, Volume 2 (Grand Rapids: Baker, 2004), 587

2. C. S. Lewis, "The Weight of Glory," in *The Weight of Glory: And Other Addresses* (New York: HarperCollins, 1949/2001), 46

3. Stark, *Victory of Reason*, 24.

4. Stark, *Victory of Reason*, 24.

5. Stark, *Victory of Reason*, 25.

6. Wayne Grudem, *Politics According to the Bible: A Comprehensive Resource for Understanding Modern Political Issues in Light of Scripture*, (Grand Rapids: Zondervan, 2010), 160.

7. John C. G. Röhl, *The Kaiser and His Court: Wilhelm II and the Government of Germany*, trans. Terrence F. Cole (Cambridge: Cambridge University Press, 1996), 211.

8. "Complete Final Debate Transcript: John McCain and Barack Obama," *Los Angeles Times*, October 15, 2008 (http://latimesblogs.latimes.com/washington/2008/10/debate-transcri.html)

9. Andrew McCarthy, "Why Obama Really Voted For Infanticide," *National Review Online*, August 22, 2008 (http://www.nationalreview.com/articles/225404/why-obama-really-voted-infanticide/andrew-c-mccarthy)

10. Peter Singer, *Rethinking Life and Death* (Oxford: Oxford University Press, 1995), 1.

11. Cited by J. Budziszewski, *What We Can't Not Know* (2nd ed., San Francisco: Ignatius, 2011), 254.

12. Donald DeMarco, "Peter Singer: Architect of the Culture of Death" (http://www.catholiceducation.org/articles/medical_ethics/me0049.html)

13. Eduard Verhagen, M.D., J.D., "The Groningen Protocol: Euthanasia in Severely Ill Newborns," *The New England Journal of Medicine*, Vol.352, No.10 (March 10, 2005), 959-62.

14. Van der Heide, et. al., "Medical end-of-life decisions made for neonates and infants

in the Netherlands," *The Lancet*, Vol.350, Issue 9073 (July 1997), 251-255 (http://www.thelancet.com/journals/lancet/article/PIIS0140673697023155/abstract)

15. Alberto Guibilini and Francesca Minerva, "After-birth abortion: why should the baby live?" *Journal of Medical Ethics* (http://jme.bmj.com/content/early/2012/03/01/medethics-2011-100411)

16. Wesley J. Smith, "Latest infanticide push about more than killing babies," *The Daily Caller*, February 29, 2012 (http://dailycaller.com/2012/02/29/latest-infanticide-push-about-more-than-killing-babies) Emphasis added.

17. Will Wilkinson, "On opinions beyond the reach of data," *The Economist*, February 8, 2012 (http://www.economist.com/blogs/democracyinamerica/2012/02/empiricism-politics)

18. Angela Franks, *Margaret Sanger's Eugenic Legacy: Control of Female Fertility*, (Jefferson, NC: McFarland, 2005), 47.

19. Margaret Sanger: The Mike Wallace Interview (http://www.hrc.utexas.edu/multimedia/video/2008/wallace/sanger_margaret_t.html)

20. "Head-to-head: Assisted suicide," *BBC News*, August 31, 2001 (http://news.bbc.co.uk/2/hi/uk_news/1518583.stm); Ira Rosofsky, "Assisted Suicide? How About a Dutch Treat?" *Psychology Today*, May 19, 2011 (http://www.psychologytoday.com/blog/adventures-in-old-age/201105/assisted-suicide-how-about-dutch-treat); Joseph P. Shapiro, "Euthanasia's Home: What the Dutch experiment can teach Americans about assisted suicide," *U.S. News & World Report*, January 5, 1997 (http://www.usnews.com/usnews/news/articles/970113/archive_005964_4.htm)

21. Van der Heide, et. al., "End-of-Life Practices in the Netherlands under the Euthanasia Act," *The New England Journal of Medicine*, Vol.356 (2007): 1957-1965 (http://www.nejm.org/doi/full/10.1056/nejmsa071143)

22. "Dutch Press Review," *Radio Netherlands Worldwide*, February 7, 2012 (http://www.rnw.nl/english/article/dutch-press-review-tuesday-7-february-2012)

23. Ian Robert Dowbiggin, *A Merciful End: The Euthanasia Movement in Modern America* (New York: Oxford University Press, 2003), xiv-xv.

24. Wesley J. Smith, "A Merciful End: The Euthanasia Movement in Modern America," *First Things* (May, 2003) (http://www.firstthings.com/article/2007/01/a-merciful-end-the-euthanasia-movement-in-modern-america-38)

25. For an eye-opening look at the 20th century eugenics movement, see Richard Coniff, "God and White Men at Yale," *Yale Alumni Magazine* (May/June 2012) (http://yalealumnimagazine.com/issues/2012_05/feature_eugenics.html)

26. George Weigel, "Child Sacrifice in 21st Century America," *First Things*, January 25, 2012 (http://www.firstthings.com/onthesquare/2012/01/child-sacrifice-in-21st-century-america)

27. Mara Hvistendahl, *Unnatural Selection: Choosing Boys Over Girls and the Consequences of a World Full of Men* (New York: PublicAffairs, 2011)

28. Jonathan V. Last, "The War Against Girls," *The Wall Street Journal*, June 24, 2011 (http://online.wsj.com/article/SB10001424052702303657404576361691165631366.html?mod=WSJ_Books_LS_Books_7)

CHAPTER THREE

ON SEXUALITY

This chapter is lengthy because it deals with an explosive topic. Explosive for two reasons. First, I am under no illusions that no matter how delicately I treat the topic of homosexuality and same-sex marriage, there are people who will accuse me of bigotry and "hate" speech. That is simply a fact of life in contemporary society, and a particularly dangerous fact of life. A culturally diverse, pluralistic society cannot long survive when the bar is set low for what counts as bigotry. Ben Stevens observes that a modern society

> will be packed with people who hold to widely divergent beliefs and values, any of which may be questioned. And the glue of this system is not that we all agree with one another but that we make a *commitment to not always equate disagreement, or even disapproval, with bigotry.*[1]

He goes on to note the irony that when the LGBT (Lesbian Gay Bisexual Transgender) movement "equates all disagreement and disapproval of itself with bigotry, and seeks to classify any question about the tenets of its own orthodoxy as hate speech" it is, in effect, "working to construct the same kind of society in which it was for so long unwelcome." In other words, the kind of culture envisioned by the LGBT movement, one in which any dissent or disapproval of their lifestyle is beyond the pale, is not an enlightened, modern, diverse society at all. It is the rejection of enlightened, modern, culturally diverse society.

I agree with Stevens, and simply reject out of hand that disapproval of homosexual conduct or same-sex marriage is by itself evidence of some deep-seated hatred or bigotry. It is certainly my hope that this chapter will show that it isn't. The truth is that evangelical Christians are constantly challenged to rethink and doubt their views on morality; it is perfectly fair to challenge the moral worldview of the LGBT movement, as personal and passionate an issue as it might be. It would certainly be an ironic thing if, immediately after extolling that "God Loves People" as his intrinsically dignified image-bearers, I launched into a chapter demonizing and dehumanizing a class of people. So let me say this at the outset. I believe that homosexual behavior is destructive and contrary to God's design. I believe that it is dehumanizing. I also believe that sins of this kind are complex and life-dominating. I think the common approach of viewing same-sex attraction as a mere matter of "choice" is insufficient. The Bible calls us "slaves of sin" for a reason. Sin is a dominating power, and same-sex attraction is no exception. As a fellow image-bearer of God, as well as a fellow sinner, I have nothing but respect and sympathy for those who are caught up in the homosexual lifestyle. I know those who don't feel "caught up" in anything might take this as condescending. But as a sinner often caught up in dominating sins of my own, the sentiment, I assure you, is sincere.

It seems to me there is an important distinction to be made between an ordinary individual and a militant or activist. I believe it is possible to strongly critique a movement, comprised of self-conscious activists with specific cultural agendas without lumping in and demonizing every individual sharing something in common with the movement. The LGBT movement qualifies as an example. As we will see, it has a very specific, intentional cultural agenda that needs to be resisted. This is not at all the same thing as imputing that agenda to each and every person engaged in the LGBT lifestyle.

The second reason sexuality is explosive is just because it is. If there is anything else in the world that can bring such high levels of joy, love, laughter, and peace, and yet at the same time be the cause of so much bitterness, pain, misery, and discord, I would like to know what it is. Sex has this kind of power because it is one of God's greatest creations. Remember how the creation account in Genesis "orders" everything for the benefit of human flourishing? The pinnacle of the account is the union of Adam and Eve: "For this reason a man will leave his father and mother and be united to his wife, and they will become one flesh" (Genesis 2:24). Because sexual union is an ideal of creation, it can be absolutely spectacular. That unfortunately means that sexual dysfunction is equally spectacular. A nuclear reactor in a controlled environment is simply amazing; but so is a nuclear meltdown, only not so positive. And sexuality is, in many ways, like a nuclear reactor. When operating according to the design parameters it is an incredibly powerful and fruitful thing. Outside of those design parameters it becomes deadly. As we will see, this is not mere hyperbole. Sexual dysfunction and frustration is often at the root human misery, as the average family law attorney will tell you. One of the most naïve sentiments today is that sex is something irrelevant to the public good. On the contrary, how a culture channels the human sex-drive is the kind of thing that makes or breaks entire civilizations.

THE BIBLE AND SEXUAL DESIGN

Genesis sets the design parameters for human sexual expression, the boundaries in which sexual fruitfulness in all its facets, physical, spiritual, mental, psychological are realized: marriage between a man and woman. And the rest of the Bible not only upholds and confirms these original design parameters, but condemns *all* deviations from this norm. That means all deviations from the norm; sexual relations of any kind outside the context of a marriage, including (but not limited to) premarital sex, adultery, rape, polygamy, bestiality, and, yes, homosexual relations. Much of the focus of this chapter will be on homosexuality. This is not because in and of itself homosexuality is a pressing civic matter. Those engaged in the behavior are (even with the often vastly inflated numbers) a very small minority in this country. It has only become a hot-button political issue because the LGBT movement has self-consciously made it a hot-button political issue in this country. As we will see, they have done this in a variety of ways, most notably in their efforts to redefine the longstanding definition of marriage as including same-sex couples and to demonize all opposition as bigoted and "homophobic." In focusing on same-sex "marriage" (quotation marks are purposeful: I believe it is a contradiction in terms) I am not in the least unaware that the biblical design for marriage is under assault in other ways, such as the easy divorce culture common, sadly, even in evangelical circles. It is true that evangelical credibility is damaged when opposing same-sex "marriage" while our own marriage culture is a disaster. It is a mistake, however, to suppose that this damaged credibility is a reason to stop opposing the assault on marriage in other ways. Armies do not stop fighting the left flank just because of a desertion problem on the right flank.

The easiest and most economical thing to do is immediately turn our attention to one classic New Testament text that addresses specifically homosexual behavior, because it so clearly articulates the concept of creational design parameters and its deviations: Romans 1. Paul's letter to the Romans has been known to be regarded in contemporary "enlightened" societies as "hate speech," and pastors have, in fact, been arrested for preaching on it! Since it is at the core of controversy, it is worthwhile to take another look at it.

The most controversial words are found in verses 26-27:

> Because of this, God gave them over to shameful lusts. Even their women exchanged natural relations for unnatural ones. In the same way the men also abandoned natural relations with women and were inflamed with lust for one another. Men committed indecent acts with other men, and received in themselves the due penalty for their perversion.

There is not too much left ambiguous or up to the imagination. As a well-trained Jew, Paul knew well what God had said about homosexuality: "If a man lies with a man as one lies with a woman, both of them have done what is detestable" (Leviticus 20:13). In Romans 1 Paul is providing an extended theological commentary on exactly why. At its most basic, sexual perversion is the result of a failure of *worship*. When human beings "exchange the truth of God for the lie and worship and serve created things rather than the Creator," (1:25), they worship and serve themselves and their immediate passions instead.

Before I expand on Paul's argument, it might be useful to address a few popular objections about the Bible's teaching with regard to homosexual conduct. Its teaching for many people has become something of an embarrassment, and they wish to tone it down. There are three ways of doing this:

1) Say that the Bible doesn't really condemn homosexuality as we know it today, but has something else in mind.

2) Point out that the Bible condemns lots of other things we don't seem to have problems with (i.e., Sabbath breaking), and use that to minimize its teaching on homosexuality.

3) Say that the Bible does condemn homosexuality but the Bible is wrong and we now know better.

A popular variation on (3) is to drive a wedge between Jesus and Paul, observing that Jesus "never said a word about homosexuality" (as former President Jimmy Carter has recently opined), and so Paul is out of step with Jesus on the matter. President Obama expressed this conviction in a campaign speech, as well: "If people find [civil unions] controversial, then I would refer them to the Sermon on the Mount, which I think, you know, is in my mind, in my faith, more central than an obscure passage in Romans."[2] And this is not a one-off campaign line, either. It is a carefully considered opinion, given that he wrote in his autobiography: "I am not willing to have the state deny American citizens a civil union [...] simply because the people they love are of the same sex—nor am I willing to accept a reading of the Bible that considers an obscure line in Romans to be more defining of Christianity than the Sermon on the Mount."[3] So Jesus' sermon is contrasted with "an obscure line" in Romans? Of course, there is nothing obscure about the book of Romans. It is only the lengthiest, most studied, and (arguably) the most cherished letter in the New Testament! The only difference between this and "the Bible is wrong and we know better" is that Jesus is invoked as agreeing with us that the Bible (Romans) is wrong and we know better.

Let me briefly address these approaches in reverse order. Number (3) and its variant is an impossible position for an evangelical Christian to take. The Bible is God's Word, and therefore cannot be wrong on such a matter, and the Bible is a singular, unified revelation of God and therefore Jesus and Paul cannot be pitted against one another. Jesus gave Paul the authority to speak for him (Acts 9:15; Galatians 1:1). And, as a matter of fact, Jesus did opine about sexuality and marriage; he pointed his listeners directly back to the original design parameters, quoting Genesis word-for-word:

> 'Haven't you read,' he replied, 'that at the beginning the Creator made them male and female,' and said, 'For this reason a man will leave his father and mother and be united to his wife, and the two will become one flesh'? So they are no longer two, but one. Therefore what God has joined together, let man not separate' (Matthew 19:4-6).

Add to this the obvious fact that Jesus was a 1st century Jew who claimed that he did *not* come to abolish the Old Testament law (Matthew 5:17), and suddenly the "silence" means exactly the opposite of what many wish it to mean. Rather than a tacit disapproval of, say, Leviticus, his silence on any given issue is a tacit approval of the law given to Moses.

Moreover, Jesus never said a word about beating one's wife, kidnapping, or molesting children. His silence, even if it were true, proves exactly... nothing. Non-evangelicals of all stripes are welcome to take the view that the Bible is wrong and we know better; but they need to be prepared to answer the question how we know better. On what rational and moral basis do we know that homosexuality is morally acceptable? It is often assumed, incessantly declared, agreement demanded as a prerequisite to be included at the cool cocktail parties, but it is never argued.

Number (2) is also common, and was made very popular by an episode of the television show *The West Wing*, in which Martin Sheen's character, President Josiah Bartlett, publicly ridicules (who else?) an evangelical Christian talk show host for her opposition to homosexuality. In his passionate diatribe, Bartlett argues (if you can call an offensive, pugnacious, humiliating, in-your-face, condescending dressing-down of a woman in public an "argument"—*West Wing* writer Aaron Sorkin has some disturbing fantasies. I'd encourage you to watch it on YouTube) that if homosexuality is immoral based on Leviticus, then so is everything else in biblical law. And that would include not eating shrimp or playing football on Sundays (Sabbath violation!), or even playing football with a pigskin![4] More recently homosexual advocate Dan Savage, speaking at a public high school, trotted out a version of this argument, claiming that we need to "get over the bulls—t in Leviticus," just like we did with the "bulls—t" about eating shellfish.[5] There is a clever website dedicated to this line of argument called "God Hates Shrimp." Everything about this is logical except that the premise is wrong: God doesn't hate shrimp.

There is something very ironic about the argument. On the one hand, liberals are always accusing evangelicals for reading the Bible overly literally, and yet it is difficult to imagine a more narrow, wooden interpretation than the idea that each and every commandment must be leveled out to the same degree of seriousness and/or have identical moral application. Truthfully, at least on this issue, evangelicals read the Bible with far more theological and literary sophistication than their liberal counterparts. The fact is that there are different kinds of laws given to Israel with different purposes. Not every command reflects a universally binding moral principle. Many were laws specifically for Israelites, and did not apply, for example, to visitors and foreigners. Many were religious ceremonial rites that centered on Israel's worship in the tabernacle and, later, the Temple. These kinds of laws, usually invoking terms like "clean" and "unclean," were object lessons for the Israelites: God was teaching them to make distinctions between holy and unholy. Living in the shadow of a tabernacle or Temple in which a holy God dwells required something of a safety manual, much like living in the shadow of a nuclear power plant requires a rather hefty safety manual. Laws concerning what kinds of foods are clean or unclean relate to religious obligations in the Temple, and are not universal moral condemnations for all time. This is why Jesus could later declare that "all foods are clean" (Mark 7:19). He was teaching that, with his arrival, the religious "object lessons" were not needed anymore.[6]

The task of interpreting the different categories of laws and whether a particular law reflects a ceremonial or strictly moral rationale is a difficult and complex area of biblical study. Theologians have wrestled with the questions for centuries, as have anthropologists more recently. It requires sophisticated and subtle strategies for interpretation, and in some cases the answer is unclear. *Homosexuality is not and never has been one of these unclear cases.* Leviticus uses the strongest word in its moral evaluation of the conduct: it is an "abomination." This is something never said about violating dietary laws or even Sabbath-breaking. This alone indicates that it is not an activity even remotely like eating shrimp or playing football.

We should also note that the section of Leviticus we are being urged to discount as an irrelevant, Stone Age, anthropological museum relic also condemns child sacrifice, rape, incest, polygamy, and bestiality. Is Dan Savage willing to call those prohibitions morally outdated "bulls—t" that we need to "get over"? Not likely. But if not, why not?

And, finally, perhaps the most common rationale for why the Bible doesn't really condemn homosexual behavior is (1): it has something in mind other than loving, committed, monogamous homosexual relationships (e.g., forcible rape). Space will not allow me to provide a lengthy refutation of this idea, but a few words should suffice. A decade ago New Testament scholar Robert A. J. Gagnon wrote the most critically-acclaimed, definitive book on this question, entitled *The Bible and Homosexual Practice*.[7] So critically-acclaimed was it that even world-renowned scholars who disagreed with him admitted that of all the material written on the topic, his was the one book that had to be dealt with.[8] For the most part it has been dealt with by completely ignoring it. Even though Gagnon utterly demolished the idea that the Bible doesn't really condemn the kind of homosexual behavior we have today, many have nevertheless recycled and reused the argument. And this recycling never involves actually answering Gagnon's analysis. Happily, not everybody recycles. Historian Louis Crompton (himself a homosexual) recognizes the reality:

> According to this interpretation, Paul's words were not directed at 'bona fide' homosexuals in committed relationships. But such a reading, however well-intentioned, seems strained and unhistorical. Nowhere does Paul or any other Jewish writer of this period imply the least acceptance of same-sex relations under any circumstances. The idea that homosexuals might be redeemed by mutual devotion would have been wholly foreign to Paul or any other Jew or early Christian.[9]

So those three objections are insufficient in evading the force of the biblical injunctions. So let us return to Romans 1. In the broader context Paul's evaluation of "ungodliness" and "wickedness" (v.18) is grounded in the doctrine of creation. Right off the bat, Paul declares that God has made himself known "since the creation of the world" (v.20). And if you look closely, the language of Genesis permeates this section of his letter: he speaks of a kind of pseudo "wisdom," which is exactly what the Serpent promised Adam and Eve (v.22); he speaks of the idolatry of worshiping images that look like "birds and animals and reptiles," three words literally quoted straight off the page of Genesis (v.23); he explicitly evaluates sin as worshiping and serving "created things rather than the Creator" (v.25); when he speaks of the sexual impurities of men and women, he does not use the common Greek words for "man" and "woman" (likely obscured in your English translation) but rather the far more uncommon terms "male" and "female," again, words directly borrowed from Genesis ("male and female he created them"); and finally, he describes the sexual conduct as "natural" and "unnatural" relations. In other words, there is a sexual design, there has been from the very beginning, and people not acting in accordance with the design are performing unnatural relations. In fact, the words translated "unnatural" literally mean "contrary to nature" (*para physin*).

Paul clearly teaches that there are sexual design parameters, and he believes that homosexual conduct is contrary to those design parameters. He is not talking about only a certain kind of homosexual relationship, whether it is pederasty or rape; he is talking about the act in and of itself. That is why he uses the terms "male" and "female," not "man" and "woman." The wrongness does not derive from social or other ethical factors such as whether the person is domineering or violent; the wrongness is determined strictly by *anatomy*. Moreover, he cannot be speaking about a situation of domination or rape, because he writes that men "were inflamed with lust for *one another*." The conduct in view is consensual.

Exclusive focus on Paul's negative critique of homosexual relations unfortunately gives the impression that perhaps he was obsessed with the topic or is perhaps unfairly or inordinately singling it out. Three things involving the broader context need to be said in response to that impression.

First, *Paul is not singling out homosexual conduct because it is the worst possible sin.* Look at the list of sins he goes on to equally condemn as "deserving of death" (v.32): wickedness, evil, greed, depravity, envy, murder, strife, deceit, malice, gossip, slander, God-hating, insolence, arrogance, boasting, disobedience to parents (!), being senseless, faithless, heartless, and ruthless. Any of those things will send you to hell just as surely as homosexual conduct. You will find this is true of other sin lists in the Bible; homosexual conduct is always included, but not singled out.

Second, *Paul's entire purpose is to condemn every single person on the face of the earth.* Seriously. Paul actually knows that a certain brand of self-righteous person, say, a member of Fred Phelps's Westboro Baptist Church holding a "God hates fags" sign, will read what he writes about the really wicked types and think, "Yeah, Paul! Sock it to 'em!" So beginning in chapter 2 he turns to that type of person and says this: "You, therefore, have no excuse, you who pass judgment on someone else, for at whatever point you judge the other, you are condemning yourself, because you who pass judgment do the same things" (Romans 2:1) It is a brilliant piece of writing. He unleashes on the pagans in chapter 1 knowing that the self-righteous will agree with him. They don't know what hit them when he gets to chapter 2.

When King David sinned grievously by committing adultery and murder, God sent a prophet named Nathan to confront him (2 Samuel 12). Nathan's gambit was brilliant. He told a story about a rich man that stole a poor person's beloved sheep, and an outraged David demanded the rich man's death. "*You* are the man!" Nathan declared. Paul's strategy is identical: he gets his self-righteous readers to agree with his condemnations of the pagans, only to declare: "*You* are the man!" This doesn't get the pagans of chapter 1 off the hook, mind you. By chapter 3 Paul's entire purpose becomes clear. He is relentlessly painting this ugly picture of humanity, Jews as well as Gentiles, so that "every mouth may be silenced and the *whole world* held accountable to God" (Romans 3:19). Paul's point in Romans 1, then, is not to just single out homosexual conduct as being particularly bad; it is one facet of an overall argument to make every single person everywhere look particularly bad. Why does he want to do that? To make every single person everywhere desperate for a Savior: Jesus Christ.

But we cannot ignore the fact that Paul does single out homosexuality here. Why? Remember from our study of Genesis that the very apex of creation, the very expression of human flourishing was for the man and woman to be united as "one flesh" and to be fruitful and multiply. Paul wants to show that humanity's rejection of God has turned everything upside-down, that the very purpose of human flourishing represented in the one-flesh union of a man and woman has been compromised. The disruption of humanity's "vertical" relationship to God has disrupted its "horizontal" relationships with one another.

Imagine that a company created a certain kind of jet, and before the first test flight they hire an outside engineering company to do an evaluation to see if it is airworthy. Imagine that the official independent engineering report details a number of trivial or ancillary problems (an indicator light here or there was not working properly, etc.) yet fails to identify the biggest, most important thing: *complete engine failure*. The company wants to know if the plane will fulfill its ultimate purpose; it would not be a very good analysis to ignore the most obvious sign that the plane isn't going to fly. Likewise, Paul is examining humanity's failure in its ultimate purpose of being fruitful and multiplying; and the sexual dysfunction homosexuality represents is sort of like "engine failure." There is literally no fruit from a same-sex union. Humanity literally cannot flourish if such practices are normative. It would mean literal extinction. Homosexuality represents "engine failure," the most extreme illustration of futility at his disposal. But Paul doesn't leave the indicator lights out, either, which is why he gives a lengthy list of sins.

In that light, it is simply the case that there is no more obvious illustration of sexual design failure than males having sexual intercourse with males or females having sexual relations with females. I realize that this has become controversial and the stuff of hate-speech codes. But sometimes the obvious needs to be said. It is not knowledge unique to electricians that the male end of the power cord only works with a female receptacle. *Everybody knows this.* Reality is what it is; the cosmos has a design. Only illusory magic formulas can deny it. Further, if one purpose of human sexuality is fruitfulness, it is not surprising that Paul focuses on sexual practices that are (and this is indisputable) fruitless.

Paul's treatment in Romans 1 is certainly negative. Without question, he takes a condemnatory tone in the interests of showing how everyone is condemned apart from the gospel of Jesus Christ. But the backdrop behind that negativity is a profoundly positive view of the human design. Remember that what the Bible is about is life.

We saw in the last chapter Mara Hvistendahl's observation that a culture with an excess of men is a very dangerous place because it breeds violence and sexual exploitation. Men do not have a healthy outlet for their sexual desires. But this can be true even in a culture with plenty of women. *Where there is no cultural expectation that sexuality be channeled into the institution of marriage, men will be unrestrained in their lusts and women will be ripe targets for exploitation and victimization.* I know that this thesis is dismissed by many as a paranoid slippery slope kind of argument, but it isn't. There is a causal relationship and it is empirically verifiable. Read that italicized sentence again. No, really. Read it again.

Now think of what has happened to the African-American family in urban centers. Completely unburdened men with no intentions toward marriage whatsoever fathering multiple children by different women, and completely burdened women saddled with multiple children by different men. The social results are extreme government dependency, fatherless children, poverty, and increasing crime. In some urban communities eight out of ten children live without a father. Everyone recognizes this as a problem. It is not the stuff of hyperventilating conservatives engaged in culture wars. Yet many progressives refuse to acknowledge one of the primary factors: the breakdown of the institution of marriage in the inner-cities. Total sexual liberation has been the mantra of progressivism for decades. When the inevitable societal consequences have now manifested themselves, they argue that the culprit is anything but total sexual liberation. It is a lack of funding, or programs, or sex education, or "morning after" pills, or condoms. It is never the cultural consequence of a relentless disregard of marriage as a human sexual ideal.

The societal consequences—cultural, economic, legal, educational, etc.— of the breakdown of marriage are well-known and indisputable. In fact, renowned sociologist Charles Murray puts it this way:

> No matter what the outcome being examined—the quality of the mother-infant relationship, externalizing behavior in childhood (aggression, delinquency, and hyperactivity), delinquency in adolescence, criminality as adults, illness and injury in childhood, early mortality, sexual decision making in adolescence, school problems and dropping out, emotional health, or any other measure of how well or poorly children do in life—the family structure that produces the best outcomes for children, on average, are two biological parents who remain married [...] *I know of no other set of important findings that are as broadly accepted by social scientists who follow the technical literature, liberal as well as conservative, and yet are so resolutely ignored by network*

news programs, editorial writers for the major newspapers, and politicians of both major political parties.[10]

Yet conservatives concerned about "family values" are constantly derided as the "anti-science" constituency. The social sciences are, as Murray explains, unanimous in the conclusion that marriage between one man and one woman is by far the ideal context for the raising up of the next generation. Progressives love to style themselves as the "reality-based" community, devoted only to "facts," yet these inconvenient facts do not seem to penetrate the filters.

Dennis Prager argues—persuasively, in my view—that the real sexual revolution occurred in ancient history with the Jewish ideal of marriage between one man and one woman.[11] He documents the sexual anarchy of the ancient pagan cultures, where women were completely marginalized and exploited, and contrasts it with Judaism. I mentioned before how revolutionary the Bible is when it includes women in its creation account as being equally the image of God, and Prager helpfully confirms the point. It is unprecedented in ancient literature to have a command like, "Honor your father *and your mother...*" The institution of marriage provided women dignity and protection. It provided men a safe, healthy, responsible, and fruitful avenue for their sex drives. This institution, more than any other, is responsible for civilization itself. Where sexual anarchy reigns, there is social dysfunction, as any given Woody Allen movie will amply illustrate. Prager's thesis is boldly stated:

> Societies that did not place boundaries around sexuality were stymied in their development. The subsequent dominance of the Western world can largely be attributed to the sexual revolution initiated by Judaism and later carried forward by Christianity.
>
> This revolution consisted of forcing the sexual genie into the marital bottle. It ensured that sex no longer dominated society, heightened

male-female love and sexuality (and thereby almost alone created
the possibility of love and eroticism within marriage), and began the
arduous task of elevating the status of women.[12]

I highly recommend reading his entire essay, which is easily accessed on
the Internet. The institution of the family is the basic adhesive of human
society, binding men and women to each other and, together, to their
children. The family is the training ground of the next generation for
participation in every facet of society and culture. The Western world has
been busy pouring acid on this arrangement for a generation, praising
sexual liberation, divorce, adultery, fornication, pornography, and, yes,
homosexuality. British anthropologist Joseph Unwin, reflecting on the
social histories of 80 different civilizations, found that when a society
strays from the sexual ethic of marriage, it deteriorates and eventually
disintegrates.[13] As I said, sexual energy is like nuclear energy: channeled in
certain ways it can be a spectacular force for good. Freed from parameters
and constraints, both are corrosive enough to destroy civilizations.

The rise of homosexuality as a legitimate lifestyle currently has the most
pressing (note: not only) political implication because of the recent
attempts to have the state redefine marriage to include same-sex couples.
These attempts have a compassionate tone of voice, as though it were
merely a matter of recognizing "true love" wherever it may be found. As
Barack Obama put it, he is unwilling to deny state-sanctioned legitimacy
to relationships "simply because the people they love are of the same sex."
This kind of rhetoric is quite juvenile, akin to the common playground
retort when a child claims to "love" something: "Why don't you *marry* it?"
Love is not, nor has it ever been, the single defining feature constituting
a marriage. A different playground rhyme gets it better: "First comes love
/ then comes marriage / then comes a baby in a baby carriage!" Marriage
is not synonymous with "love."

The government does not hand out "friendship" licenses, loving as that relationship might be. They do not issue "roommate" licenses, regardless of how close the pals or girlfriends are. Nor do they give out licenses for sisters or brothers to cohabitate, doting and faithful as they might be. They give out marriage licenses. Why? Because the sexual union of one man and one woman is the relationship that (in the vast majority of circumstances) produces children. And children have rights and parents have responsibilities. It is this fact, and this fact alone, that makes this arrangement, and not any other social arrangement, subject to governmental sanction and regulation. This relationship must be codified in law—parents bound to each other and both of them together bound to their children. No man has any kind of legal claim on a woman married to another man, and vice-versa, and no person has a claim on somebody else's child. It is the legally codified institution of marriage that sanctions and protects these relationships and the freedoms and responsibilities they entail. "Love" does not a marriage make.

But the LGBT movement's lexicon is full of exactly the kinds of sentimental words that appeal to Americans: "loving," "monogamous," "tolerance," "rights," "fairness," "equality," and so forth. What is lost on many Americans is that this rhetoric is self-consciously designed to appeal to them. Behind the rhetoric is an agenda on a far grander scale than simply giving "equal rights" to lesbians, gays, bisexuals, and transgender people. The ultimate goal is to transcend marriage itself as a backward, archaic, and oppressive Judeo-Christian institution.

MAGIC FORMULAS

You do not need to take my word for it. In 1987 two influential homosexual activists, Marshall Kirk and Hunter Madsen, published an article entitled, "Overhauling Straight America," and followed it up with a book called After the Ball: How America Will Conquer Its Fear and Hatred of Gays in the 90's. In these works they very clearly outline a plan of action in six parts:

1. Talk about gays and gayness as loudly and often as possible.

2. Portray gays as victims, not aggressive challengers.

3. Give homosexual protectors a "just" cause.

4. Make gays look good.

5. Make the victimizers look bad.

6. Solicit funds (particularly from corporate America).

This six-point strategy has been played to near-perfection in the intervening years. The playbook ought to be recognizable to anyone who has been paying attention over the past two decades, and for a detailed look at how each of these proposals have been carried out readers should consult *The Homosexual Agenda*, by Alan Sears and Craig Osten.[14] Of particular importance for our purposes is number (3). The decision to cast the same-sex "marriage" debate in terms of "civil rights" was a calculated decision. Kirk and Madsen knew that Americans naturally respond to arguments about fairness.

Here is something even more obscure to most Americans: the elite intellectuals of the LGBT movement *have no intention of conforming to a social institution like marriage*. Yes, they pursue the goal of enshrining same-sex "marriage" in law, but this is a half-way house to the real goal, which is to get beyond the old "power structures," one of which is marriage. The late Paula Ettelbrick, a pioneer in the LGBT quest for legal recognition, was quite candid:

Being queer is more than setting up house, sleeping with a person of the same gender, and seeking state approval for doing so. It is an identity, a culture with many variations. It is a way of dealing with the world [...] Being queer means pushing the parameters of sex, sexuality, and family, and in the process transforming the very fabric of society [....] We must keep our eyes on the goals of providing true alternatives to marriage and of radically reordering society's view of family.[15]

"Transforming the very fabric of society." "Radically reordering society's view of family." These are the goals of academic "queer theory," which has its roots in Continental postmodern philosophy, particularly the deconstructionism of French philosopher Michel Foucault. The entire point of queer theory, even according to Foucault himself, was to refuse to be "normalized" into existing sexual power structures like marriage. So while many LGBT intellectuals support same-sex "marriage," they do so somewhat begrudgingly, keeping in mind that it is not at all the ultimate goal. David Halperin explains that this is what Foucault himself desired:

In the end, although I think Foucault would have been perfectly delighted by the push for gay marriage, I also think he would have wanted the gay movement to seize this opportunity to promote and to valorize *many different forms of relationships between two or more people* [....] I think he would have wanted the gay marriage debate to open a space for the discussion of a *plurality of possibilities for different kinds of relationships* that could be promoted alongside of marriage.[16]

Note well: the goal is for a societal "inventiveness" for sexual relationships, and what is envisioned is not something restricted to two people, but two "or more." Mark Kingston explains in even more detail:

In light of this general questioning of the norms that structure our relationships, it might even be argued that it no longer makes sense to talk in terms of homosexual and heterosexual relationships, if what we mean by that is that these relationships both have their own intrinsic and immutable characteristics. Rather, we should talk about a multitude of *sui generis* relationships that are just, as it happens, between a man and a woman, or between two women or two men, or between more than two people. This is what David M. Halperin means when he says that 'The future Foucault envisages for us is not exclusively or categorically gay. But it is definitely queer.'[17]

Readers may be forgiven for being ignorant of discussions of this kind in academic "queer theory" because the gap is wide between this kind of theorizing and the popular case being made for "gay rights." Behind the rhetoric of "equality" and "justice" is a clear agenda that has no intention of honoring the institution of marriage at all. The whole point, as these excerpts make clear, is to get beyond the chains and fetters of marriage and re-envision human sexuality at its root. This is not a secret. Academics openly acknowledge and discuss these things in journals and conferences to which the average person has little access (much less interest). Marriage is, in this progressive worldview, a *purely arbitrary and oppressive social convention* that needs to be discarded in favor of newly-invented, or *sui generis* (as Kingston terms it, meaning "unique" or "one of a kind") relationships that one cannot predetermine or define.

Compare all this to the outrage unleashed on Senator Rick Santorum when he had the temerity to point out that, on the logic of the LGBT movement, polygamy is next up for legal recognition. "Bigot" and "homophobe" were the very mildest epithets hurled his way, and the rest cannot be printed. Yet he was saying nothing other than what Foucault, Ettelbrick, Halperin, Kingston, and many, many others in the academic guild of queer theory have been advocating from the start. Santorum's problem was not that he misrepresented the LGBT movement; his problem is that he publicly identified the exact truth. The ivory tower chatter was just broadcast to Main Street, and Santorum quickly found himself a target of the politics of personal destruction.

It is helpful at this point to remember the distinction I made between individuals and activists. I have no doubt there are many homosexual and lesbian couples who really do love each other and want to be "married," although, it should be noted, the statistics clearly indicate that this is an incredibly small minority.[18] They themselves may be (in fact, likely are) quite unaware of the deeper philosophical implications being discussed and plotted in "queer" academic circles. But recognizing this is not an argument for same-sex "marriage," for it only indicates that they themselves have been influenced by Kirk and Madsen's six-point strategy. They have come to strongly believe this is a matter of "civil rights" and "equality." They may believe it is just a matter of equal inclusion into the already existing structural institution of marriage, but in this they are just as deceived as the heterosexual community to which the propaganda campaign was aimed. The intellectual elites of the LGBT movement want the institution of marriage destroyed and replaced with heretofore unknown, newly-invented sexual relationships. The first strategic step in doing so is redefining the institution to include same-sex couples. It is the crowbar designed to provide all the leverage needed. This means that as sympathetic as we might be to the deep sincerity or noble motives of this or that particular homosexual or lesbian couple, it is not a reason to embrace same-sex "marriage." A Trojan Horse may look like a magnificent gift, and the people delivering it may be unwitting and truly well-meaning. That doesn't make it any less a Trojan Horse.

The example of what happened to Rick Santorum when he pointed out that the trajectory of same-sex marriage entails polygamy helpfully illustrates the next piece of the LGBT agenda: the quest for public approval and official sanction of the LGBT lifestyle necessarily involves not just disagreement with the opposition, but the *silencing* of opposition. The co-chair of President Obama's LGBT Leadership Council, Stampp

Corbin, put it this way: "The most insidious word that is constantly used in our circles is tolerance [....] I do not want to be tolerated. What I want, and I hope the [LGBT] community at large wants, is acceptance. That's right, approval and respect of my orientation." If Corbin gets his wish and homosexual unions are given legally privileged status, then we know what follows because it has already happened in many places around the world: public opposition, particularly religious opposition, will be increasingly criminalized. Canada and many European countries have "hate-speech" laws and "Human Rights Commissions" whose goals include rooting out anti-homosexual bigotry among pastors,[19] comedians,[20] and anyone else who dares offend the LGBT lifestyle. Just recently a shopping mall in Los Angeles banned boxing champion (and devout Roman Catholic) Manny Pacquaio from the premises for the unacceptable act of speaking out against same-sex "marriage" in a published interview. Under that standard, the 52% of Californians who voted for Proposition 8 likewise would be banned from the mall. Of course, that is impractical, not to mention economically disastrous; it is much easier to make an example of Pacquaio to chill dissent.

This collision between the legal sanction of homosexuality and religious opposition is, frankly, inevitable. Those who believe that sanctioning same-sex "marriage" will in the long run soften the social conflict over homosexuality, much like the passage of the Civil Rights Act of 1964 did with racial tensions, are quite mistaken. David French points out that "the civil rights movement depended on Christians for its success. Martin Luther King, Jr.'s argument as a Christian to his fellow Christians was overwhelmingly compelling and grounded in the core truths of scripture. That same religious argument is simply not available here [...]."[21] In other words, while Martin Luther King, Jr. could appeal to the Bible to condemn racism (and thus win over evangelical Christians), there is no such avenue available for the LGBT community. Evangelical Christians will continue to oppose the mainstreaming of same-sex unions whether they are granted legal sanction or not. And it ought to be somewhat alarming that everywhere same-sex "marriage" has been embraced, there has been a corresponding stifling of religious dissent. R. R. Reno puts his finger precisely on this alarming aspect to the same-sex "marriage" equals "civil rights" argument:

> To merge sexual liberation into the civil-rights movement dramatically raises the stakes in public debate. The Selma analogy makes traditional views of sexual morality as noxious as racism, and in so doing encourages progressives to adopt something like a total-war doctrine. The implication is that people who hold such views should have no voice in American society and that homosexuality should be aggressively affirmed in our public and private institutions, while dissent is punished.[22]

Chai Feldblum, a Georgetown law professor and President Obama-appointed member of the Equal Employment Opportunity Commission, candidly admits the inevitability of this conflict: "When we pass a law that says you may not discriminate on the basis of sexual orientation, we are burdening those who have an alternative moral assessment of gay men and lesbians." And she is also candid about who should win this conflict. When religious liberty and sexual liberty collide, she says:

> *I'm having a hard time coming up with a case in which religious liberty should win* [....] Sexual liberty should win in most cases. There can be a conflict between religious liberty and sexual liberty, but in almost all cases the sexual liberty should win because that's the only way that the dignity of gay people can be affirmed in any realistic manner."[23]

There is in principle a necessary and inevitable relationship between the LGBT cultural agenda and the diminishing of religious liberty; this conflict cannot be wished away. And wherever same-sex "marriage" has prevailed, hate-crimes violations, fines, arrests, and jail time for religious dissenters has followed. In other words, Feldblum gets her wish: sexual liberty trumps religious liberty.

To summarize thus far, while progressivism publicly couches everything in seemingly benign notions like "tolerance" and "equal rights," the ultimate aim (regardless of whether everyone involved in the LGBT lifestyle is aware of it) is to dismantle the old, oppressive, and archaic norm of marriage. Just as notions of human dignity and life are viewed as negotiable, relative, socially-constructed illusions that may be reprogrammed like software instead of built-in hardware, so also with human sexuality and the institution of marriage. Jonah Goldberg writes that the progressive pragmatists of the 20th century "assumed that human nature had an expiration date—and that date was yesterday."[24] That certainly has not changed.

LOSING A GENERATION?

In May of this year (2012) the state of North Carolina passed an amendment to their state constitution legally defining marriage as between one man and one woman. Blogger Rachel Held Evans, a professing Christian, was quite distraught by this. She entitled her post "How to Win a Culture War and Lose a Generation." She writes:

> *My generation is tired of the culture wars. We are tired of fighting, tired of vain efforts to advance the Kingdom through politics and power, tired of drawing lines in the sand, tired of being known for what we are against, not what we are for.*

> And when it comes to homosexuality, we no longer think in the black-and-white categories of the generations before ours. We know too many wonderful people from the LGBT community to consider homosexuality a mere 'issue.' These are people, and they are our

friends. When they tell us that something hurts them, we listen. And Amendment One hurts like hell.[25]

Rachel is exactly the second kind of person for whom I am writing this book: the younger evangelical Christian tired of their parents' politics and increasingly swayed by the political worldview of progressivism. I want to close this chapter by addressing some of her themes because I think they are sincere and worth considering.

First, if by "not thinking in the black-and-white categories" of earlier generations she means categories like "sin" and "righteousness," then there is not much I can write that will be persuasive. But if you are a reader that knows intuitively that the Bible does define certain things in "black-and-white" categories, I hope my reflections will prove helpful to you. If an entire generation of evangelical youth does not believe in the moral categories of right and wrong, then we are not "losing" them; they are already nowhere to be found. But I happen to believe Rachel is exaggerating.

Rachel views the issue of same-sex "marriage" just as the LGBT movement wants her to view it. She claims to view it not just as "an issue," which would lead one to believe that she understands the broader worldview implications (the roots of the forest) instead of just the isolated question (a single tree). But this is mistaken. There is no indication that she understands the underlying philosophy undergirding the progressive LGBT political agenda. It is entirely a sentimental recognition that "these are people," "our friends," and "they hurt." I am not unsympathetic. It is my belief that many homosexuals and lesbians themselves are unaware of the broader worldview implications involved. The six-point strategy outlined by Kirk and Madsen for making religious "bigots" the aggressors and the LGBT community the victims has not just persuaded people like Rachel; it has persuaded nearly everyone. Propaganda is not a laser-guided "smart" weapon that only affects some small slice of a populace. So for Rachel and others it is Christians who are "drawing lines in the sand" and defining themselves by what they are against rather than what they are for.

This is why marriage amendments like California's Proposition 8 or North Carolina's Amendment One seem like evangelical Christians "picking on" the LGBT community. This is simply not the case. In her post, Rachel even claims that there is no possible reason for the amendment other than to purposely alienate homosexuals and lesbians. This is ignorance. These state referendums began because LGBT legal advocates were seeking legal recognition by bypassing democratic processes altogether and obtaining legal judgments from the judicial branch of state governments. Popular referendums were one way of responding to a culture war, not initiating one. Moreover, another legal strategy self-consciously employed by LGBT activists (note the word) is to get "married" in one state that allows it, return home and force, say, North Carolina to honor their "marriage" under the full faith and credit clause of the U.S. Constitution. State marriage amendments are designed, in other words, to preclude the possibility of having same-sex marriage imposed on a state without any representation or vote of any kind. There is a highly relevant, legitimate legal reason for such amendments that have nothing to do with singling out and "picking on" the LGBT community. And while she might respond that the Federal Defense of Marriage Act (DOMA) already precludes this legal scenario, it would overlook that the Obama Administration is passively seeking to undermine DOMA by not defending it in the courts.

Another concern she articulates is a common one, and it involves pitting the "gospel" against "politics." She is tired of "vain attempts to advance the Kingdom through politics and power." No matter how many times it is said and no matter how many different ways it can be said, it is still a false dichotomy. I remember during my seminary days attending a lecture on the role of Christians in civil matters. The professor was arguing for the need of a broad moral consensus in society and the legitimacy of Christians engaging in matters of politics. Part of "loving our neighbors" means, among other things, seeking their social and cultural *well-being*. A classmate of mine was baffled by this and asked me: "So I shouldn't mind if my neighbors go to hell, just so long as they're 'good' people?" He was implying that anything less than individual gospel conversions to Christ had nothing to do with the Kingdom of God! They were equivalent to Rachel's "vain efforts" to advance the Kingdom through "politics and power."

I have seen this sentiment expressed innumerable times on Internet comment threads and Facebook posts, always by disillusioned younger Christians. Somehow, according to this line of (non)thinking, caring about politics and public policy means not truly caring about people. It is always gospel or politics. But a second's thought shows this to be nonsense. Of course I want my neighbors to become Christians. But in the event that doesn't happen (I am not God, after all), I want them to have wonderful lives, not miserable ones. Contrary to my seminary classmate, it makes a great deal of real-world, practical difference whether my non-Christian neighbor (who may well be going to hell) is an upstanding citizen, faithfully married with wonderful, well-adjusted children, and a successful career or whether he shipwrecks his life and the lives of everyone around him. I would argue that if all I cared about was my neighbor's life and happiness in the *next world* while ignoring his or her life and happiness in the *present world* I would be the dictionary definition of an uncaring person. Seeking and promoting the kind of society that brings happiness and prosperity to my neighbors and their children and their children's children is not at odds with the gospel of Jesus Christ!

Another common objection to Christian opposition to same-sex "marriage" is an observation I touched on before: Christians have little credibility on the marriage issue. After all, who went along with no-fault divorce? Who largely tolerates heterosexual cohabitation and adultery? Whose divorce rates and extramarital sexual activity positively mirrors that of the wider world? The Christian community. These facts are then translated into the conclusion that Christians ought to stop opposing same-sex "marriage" until such time as they take marriage seriously in these other ways. I agree that Christians need to take marriage seriously in these other ways, but the further conclusion simply does not follow. To return to a metaphor I offered earlier: an army may be having a widespread desertion problem on the right flank, but that is no reason to surrender on the left.

Finally, I know that the optics sometimes look like Christians are somehow "obsessed" with homosexuality and marriage. We can appear narrow-minded and mean-spirited, and perhaps some of us are—for that we should repent. But I do think there is great wisdom in a famous quote falsely attributed to Martin Luther:

> If I profess with the loudest voice and clearest exposition every portion of the truth of God except precisely that little point which the world and the devil are at that moment attacking, I am not confessing Christ, however boldly I may be professing Christ.

Marriage today is "precisely that little point" under concerted attack, and Christians should fight for the institution regardless of their failures.

Marriage is a gift of God for human prosperity and flourishing. It is a public social good. We should refuse to be shamed into abandoning it.

---

1. Ben Stevens, "LGBT: An Open-Minded Movement?" *First Things*, March 19, 2012 (http://www.firstthings.com/onthesquare/2012/03/lgbt-an-open-minded-movement)

2. Senator Barack Obama in a campaign speech in Nelsonville, Ohio, March 2008 (http://www.wtap.com/news/headlines/16161977.html)

3. Barack Obama, *The Audacity of Hope* (New York: Crown, 2006), 222.

4. (http://www.youtube.com/watch?v=rWuXpfXSl5Y)

5. (http://www.youtube.com/watch?v=alXxsKLVofM)

6. For an outstanding and readable assessment of this issue, see Tim Keller, "Old Testament Law and The Charge of Inconsistency," *Redeemer Report* (June 2012) (http://redeemer.com/news_and_events/newsletter/?aid=363)

7. Robert A. J. Gagnon, *The Bible & Homosexual Practice: Texts and Hermeneutics* (Nashville: Abingdon Press, 2001)

8. Legendary biblical scholar James Barr wrote: "This is a brilliant, original, and highly important work, displaying meticulous biblical scholarship, and indispensable even for those who disagree with the author."

9. Louis Crompton, *Homosexuality & Civilization* (Cambridge, Mass: Harvard University Press, 2003), 114.

10. Charles Murray, *Coming Apart: The State of White America*, 1960-2010 (NY: Crown Forum, 2012), 158. Emphasis added.

11. Dennis Prager, "Judaism's Sexual Revolution: Why Judaism Rejected Homosexuality" *Catholic Education Resource Center* (http://catholiceducation.org/articles/homosexuality/h00003.html)

12. Prager, "Judaism's Sexual Revolution."

13. Joseph Daniel Unwin, *Sexual Regulations and Cultural Behavior* (Trona, CA: Frank M. Darrow, 1969, USA reprint), 19-20.

14. Alan Sears and Craig Osten, *The Homosexual Agenda* (Nashville: Broadman & Holman 2003)

15. Paula Ettelbrick, "Since When is Marriage a Path to Liberation?" OUT/LOOK, FALL 1989, reprinted in *Lesbians, Gay Men, and the Law*, ed. Wm. Rubenstein, 402,403,405.

16. "Foucault, Gay Marriage, and Gay and Lesbian Studies in the United States: An Interview with David Halperin," *Sexuality Research & Social Policy* Vol.1, No.3 (September 2004): 35-36. Emphasis added.

17. Mark Kingston, "Subversive Friendships: Foucault on Homosexuality and Social Experimentation," *Foucault Studies* No.7, (September 2009): 14-15.

18. Charles C.W. Cooke, "The Gay Divorcees," *National Review Online*, May 15, 2012 (http://www.nationalreview.com/articles/299944/gay-divorcees-charles-c-w-cooke#)

19. See, for example, the case of Swedish Pastor Ake Green (http://www.washingtonpost.com/wp-dyn/articles/A45538-2005Jan28.html)

20. No, this is not a joke. Comedian Guy Earle and the restaurant at which he performed were fined $22,500 for offending a lesbian couple. (http://www.dailymail.co.uk/news/article-1379653/Comedian-Guy-Earle-Zestys-restaurant-owner-22-500-Lorna-Pardy-lesbian-jokes-Vancouver-Canada.html)

21. David French, "The Long-Term Future of Gay Marriage: Stalemate," *National Review Online*, May 10, 2012 (http://www.nationalreview.com/corner/299599/long-term-future-gay-marriage-debate-stalemate-david-french)

22. R. R. Reno, "The Selma Analogy," *First Things* (May, 2012), 5.

23. Maggie Gallagher, "Banned in Boston: The Coming Conflict Between Same-Sex Marriage and Religious Liberty," *The Weekly Standard*, Vol.11, No.33 (May 15, 2006) (http://www.weeklystandard.com/Content/Public/Articles/000/000/012/191kgwgh.asp?page=1) Emphasis added.

24. Jonah Goldberg, *The Tyranny of Clichés: How the Left Cheats in the War of Ideas* (NY: Sentinel, 2012), 52.

25. Rachel Held Evans, "How to Win a Culture War and Lose a Generation," May 9, 2012 (http://rachelheldevans.com/win-culture-war-lose-generation-amendment-one-north-carolina)

PART TWO

PROSPERITY

CHAPTER FOUR

GOD LOVES PROSPERITY

In Part One we explored how Christianity informs an evangelical political approach to issues of life and sexuality. We found that God loves people and wants them to "be fruitful and to multiply." The only way for such flourishing to occur is to act in accord with God's design: that human beings have intrinsic dignity and value as divine image-bearers, and that sexual fruitfulness occurs within the context of marriage. We saw that political progressivism is built on the antithesis of this. The value and dignity of human beings is measured by some external and arbitrary standard created by elites (such as economic value to the collective) and sexual fruitfulness is redefined as complete, autonomous sexual freedom without order or limitation. As we saw, these twin convictions actually serve to dehumanize people, and therefore in principle do not contribute to human flourishing. Nor have they, as a matter of historical fact, contributed to human flourishing.

In Part Two we will continue to see the relevance of a Christian view for economic issues. Not only does Christianity accord dignity and value to human life and sexuality, but it gives meaning and significance to their labor. In addition to being fruitful and multiplying (sex and marriage), God wants people to "rule and subdue" the world and to reap the benefits of labor. God does not just love people; he loves prosperity.

This way of putting it is provocative, and there are certainly ways of misinterpreting it. Let me dispense with one possible misinterpretation straight away. I will be the first in line to condemn the burgeoning "health-and-wealth" gospel of so many charlatan preachers who assure their congregants that God wants them to be rich and that their material prosperity is a one-to-one measuring stick for the purity of their faith. That is a terrible (soul killing!) distortion of the Christian gospel, and one that I vehemently oppose (c.f., 1 Timothy 6:5: "[...] men of corrupt mind, who have been robbed of the truth, and who think that godliness *is a means to financial gain*"). But I think that sometimes critics overcorrect and unwittingly drive off the other side of the road. They suppose that God is somehow opposed to material prosperity as such, leading to the equally false notion that one's material poverty is a sign of God's favor.

Now, recognizing that opposition to wealth has a lengthy tradition in Christianity, I will readily admit that there is a way of being rich that is displeasing to God. But I will insist that it *isn't the riches themselves.* One of the most familiar Bible verses in our culture is also one of the most thoroughly abused (a close second to "Let he who is without sin cast the first stone"): "Money is the root of all evil." The only problem is that St. Paul wrote nothing of the kind! He actually wrote: "For the *love of money* is a root of *all kinds of evil*" (1 Timothy 6:10). There's a world of difference between money and the *love* of money. One is a thing; the other is an affection and/or motivation. Money is not the problem;

idolatry, the worship of money, is the problem. That is why Jesus put it in terms of religious devotion when he said, "for where your treasure is, there your heart will be also" (Matthew 6:21; c.f., Psalm 49:6; Proverbs 11:28; Mark 10:24-25). It is at the level of the heart's deepest motivation that "You cannot serve both God and Money" (Matthew 6:24). The First and Tenth Commandments are beautiful bookends, and intimately related. If we break the Tenth, "You shall not covet," we are also breaking the First: "You shall have no other gods before me." And if we break the First, nothing will stop us from breaking the Tenth, too. Money and morals are inextricably linked, and one of the problems in our day is denying this. People pretend that virtue is irrelevant to the economic marketplace, which they see as a dispassionate realm of strict cause and effect where heart motivations are irrelevant. Well, something blew up in the fall of 2008, and it is obtuse to not see lots and lots of immoral causes at the root of it.

It ought to be obvious, but, sadly, sometimes the obvious needs to be pointed out: poverty is not a good thing. When the Bible says that God has compassion on the poor, it is hardly because poverty is an ideal condition! Far from it! Scarcity is not the biblical ideal. It was not in God's original blueprints. After all, he placed Adam and Eve in a luxurious garden. There is a reason "wilderness" is a universally bad thing in the Bible. It is the opposite of cultivation, dominion, and prosperity. It is a place of insecurity, chaos, danger, and want. Rather than ruling over it, people are generally helpless in the wilderness. Scarcity is the exact opposite of the human design. Poverty and helplessness in the face of a cruel, uncaring world is the opposite of dominion, rule, and flourishing in the world.

The wilderness is where God chose to test the Israelites for 40 years. As a place of insecurity, it was ideal for people to learn utter dependence on God. Likewise, Jesus himself spent 40 days in the wilderness being tempted by the Devil to stop trusting God. The message of the wilderness, the message of poverty and scarcity, is that lasting human flourishing does not come from self-reliance. It comes from trusting in God. As we will see, this is one reason why an evangelical political worldview should not be confused with radical libertarianism (e.g., Ayn Rand), which makes self-interest and independence the highest virtues and rejects the very concepts of dependence and altruism. But the very first Psalm highlights the contrast between the person who puts his delight in God and the wicked person who does not. And the contrast is deliberately put in terms of fruitfulness and prosperity and fruitlessness and poverty: The man who delights in the law of the Lord is "like a tree planted by streams of water, which yields its fruit in season and whose leaf does not wither. Whatever he does prospers" (Psalm 1:3; c.f., 112:1-3) The following words are striking: "Not so the wicked!" God's desire for his people, as it was for Adam and Eve, is prosperity, not poverty.

I will get to how we define prosperity in a moment. But for now, we should simply notice that there is a connection between trusting God and prosperity. And that is the fractionally small element of truth in the health-and-wealth gospel. Where they go wrong is to assume that this connection is automatic and uninterrupted by the Fall. The connection between faith and prosperity is not (and never was) a physical law of direct cause-and-effect. It does not operate like deterministic Karma. God is a person, not a Genie to be manipulated. There are spectacular examples in the Bible of faithful people who suffered intensely (chief among them Jesus Christ himself, the "author and perfecter of faith" - Hebrews 11:2), even materially rich people who, despite their great faith, became impoverished by God's inscrutable will (e.g., Job). But that should not obscure that God did establish a connection: human beings were created to be his image, and that entailed their living in paradise. Sin has disrupted this connection, obviously, but that was the original design. And part of trusting in God in the midst of this fallen world is to understand his designs: his design for the world, his design for us, and his design for prosperity, and seeking, as far as we are able, to recover and live according to those designs. We will see that progressivism, as with life and sexuality, also rejects the creational designs in favor of "magic formulas" when it comes to economic theory. And that is why progressivism has never, as a matter of historical fact, produced material prosperity.

The critique of wealth in the Christian view is not really a critique of the "stuff." It is a critique of how the stuff is used: "To be rich is not a matter of having, but of using riches for the tasks of justice," writes the ancient Christian writer Lactantius.[1] Thinking that the material world is itself evil or something to be disparaged is the currency of pagan religion (e.g., Platonism, Gnosticism, Hinduism, Buddhism); Christianity is a religion that affirms the material (e.g., the resurrection of the body). This (ironically enough for those who view Christianity as opposed to material prosperity) is one major reason why modern capitalism developed in the first place, and only truly developed in the Western world: Christianity, unlike other major religions, uniquely valued the material world. That deserves repeating: one major reason for the explosion of economic prosperity in the Western world is because Christianity, the bedrock foundation of Western thought, did not make "stuff" the problem. This is very much unlike other religions that regard the material world as something we need to escape or transcend. The elites in classical Greece and Rome certainly took a dim view of commerce and preferred lives of leisure and contemplation. Plutarch regarded any activity ministering to the needs of life as "ignoble and vulgar."[2]

So if the trouble is not the stuff, what is it? The Bible's critique of wealth stems from the fact that people who have resources have a unique and heightened temptation to trust in the "stuff" (or their own abilities to get the stuff) rather than God. They worship the gifts, not the Giver. On the other hand, people languishing in the wilderness, completely helpless and without resources, do not typically have this temptation. After leading the Israelites through the wilderness, when they were on the very threshold of a land "flowing with milk and honey" (and God doesn't love prosperity?), God warned them of what would be their number one temptation:

> When you have eaten and are satisfied, praise the LORD your God for the good land he has given you [....] Otherwise, when you eat and are satisfied, when you build fine houses and settle down, and when your herds and flocks grow large and your silver and gold increase and all you have is multiplied, then your heart will become proud and you will forget the LORD your God, who brought you out of Egypt, out of the land of slavery [....] You may say to yourself, 'My power and the strength of my hands have produced this wealth for me.' But remember the LORD your God, for it is he who gives you the ability to produce wealth, and so confirms his covenant, which he swore to your forefathers, as it is today. (Deuteronomy 8:10-18)

Wealth is clearly not the problem. Self-sufficiency is the problem.

But this is a fallen world. Prosperity does not come easily. The ground is cursed with thorns and thistles. Scarcity and poverty seems more the norm for human beings than prosperity. While an overstatement, there a great deal of truth in science fiction author Robert Heinlein's humorous observation:

> Throughout history, poverty is the normal condition of man. Advances which permit this norm to be exceeded—here and there, now and then—are the work of an extremely small minority, frequently

despised, often condemned, and almost always opposed by all right-thinking people. Whenever this tiny minority is kept from creating, or (as sometimes happens) is driven out of a society, the people then slip back into abject poverty. This is known as 'bad luck.'[3]

If God had originally intended prosperity, and the historical status quo has been widespread poverty, are we to conclude that God changed his agenda? Does he continue to have plans for prosperity, or did he give up on it after Adam and Eve rejected his lavish generosity in the garden? It is clearly the former. His ultimate plan for the end of time is a renewed creation, the realization of the original flourishing intended for Adam and Eve. St. John saw a vision of this "New Jerusalem":

> Then the angel showed me the river of the water of life, as clear as crystal, flowing from the throne of God and of the Lamb down the middle of the great street of the city. On each side of the river stood the tree of life, bearing twelve crops of fruit, yielding its fruit every month. And the leaves of the tree are for the healing of the nations. No longer will there be any curse. The throne of God and of the Lamb will be in the city, and his servants will serve him. (Revelation 22:1-3).

The reference to the "Tree of Life," of course, is a direct reference to the eternal life originally offered in the Garden of Eden, and the imagery of the fruitfulness of that tree directly echoes Psalm 1. God's plan is to fulfill that original plan (not dispense with it) through the One who ultimately delighted in God's law: Jesus Christ, the "Lamb" of whom John speaks.

This is all well and good, you might say. God originally designed things for prosperity (Genesis, Garden of Eden) and he is committed to bringing about the ultimate human flourishing at the end of time (Revelation, New Jerusalem). What does that have to do with right now? If ultimate human flourishing is promised not in the here-and-now but in the hereafter, what should we think about poverty and scarcity now?

Sure, the theme of material prosperity dominates the vision of both the beginning and the end, but does the Bible have anything to say about it during the time between the Garden and the City? I believe it does. As John Schneider writes in his superb book, *The Good of Affluence: Seeking God in a Culture of Wealth:*

> [I]t is a fundamental biblical theme that material prosperity (rightly understood) is the condition that God envisions for all human beings. It describes the condition that God desired for human beings when he created the world. It describes the condition that God has in view for human beings in eternity. And it describes the condition that God (circumstances being right) desires for human beings now. In my view, being affluent in a certain way—I call it 'delight'—indeed reflects the good created order of God.[4]

I believe Schneider is right. The Bible has much to say about wealth and prosperity in the here-and-now, and there are themes I want to explore that should inform an evangelical approach to economics.

PROSPERITY REMAINS POSSIBLE

While I have already touched on it, it is worthwhile to consider it further: even after the Fall, prosperity is possible. Ultimately this is because of who God is. It is entirely his prerogative what to do with rebellious humanity after the Fall, those who gather together and conspire to throw off his constraints. But, as we saw in Chapter One, he loves people. He loves them so much he didn't scrap his plans for them, but rather executed a plan for their restoration. Jesus didn't just tell his people that they must "love their enemies" because it was a nice moral sentiment. He told them to love their enemies because that is, first and foremost, who God is! God does not just love people, he even loves people who are at odds with him. As St. Paul puts it, "God demonstrates his own love for us in this: While we were still sinners, Christ died for us" (Romans 5:8).

Now, it is a truly remarkable thing that the Bible does not completely restrict God's loving disposition only to Christian believers. As rock band U2 puts it in their song "City of Blinding Lights": "Blessings not just for the ones who kneel. Luckily." In the Sermon on the Mount, Jesus said: "Love your enemies and pray for those who persecute you, that you may be sons of your Father in heaven. He causes his sun to rise on the evil and the good, and sends rain on the righteous and the unrighteous" (Matthew 5:44-45). In the agrarian world of the first century, sun and rain are euphemisms for material well-being. Sun and rain are what produce the chief economic commodity of the time: crops. Jesus is teaching here that God's continued material blessings on humanity are motivated by his love. They are daily reminders that God loves his enemies. Jesus is teaching that the children need to imitate their Father. In fact, he goes on to say, "Be perfect, as your Father in heaven is perfect." Loving one's enemies is a creaturely imitation of a divine perfection.

Now, Scripture elsewhere makes abundantly clear that this blessing on the good and evil, righteous and unrighteous, will not continue forever. There is a final judgment and a heaven and hell. Contrary to the picture of a warm and fuzzy, feel-good Jesus in much sentimental theology, this same Jesus was the most outspoken teacher of hell the world has ever known, even in this same sermon (c.f., Matthew 5:22, 30; 7:13, 20-23; 12:36-37; 25:31-46)! The love that Jesus describes toward the unrighteous is "the riches of his kindness, tolerance and patience" and is designed to "lead to repentance" (Romans 2:4). Sadly, many remain unmoved by God's generosity and refuse to repent. But that in no way changes the fact that God is generous! He loves people, and he loves prosperity. He made them both. And he made them for each other.

The natural connection between being God's image and fruitfulness has been frustrated by the fall. It is only by the "sweat of the brow," dealing with "thorns and thistles" that the earth will give its abundance. But it still gives its abundance. Every material blessing is an undeserved blessing, a clear case of God loving his enemies. If the accounts of God's creation in Genesis, his new creation in Revelation, and his continued blessing in the present teach anything, it is this: God is not a miser. He does not hoard his wealth. That is exactly what the serpent wanted Adam and Eve to believe: that God was withholding something from them. So focused on that one, single, solitary fruit, they became oblivious to the luxurious and rich garden around them.

And we are often no different. We, too, tend to think that somehow God is unjustly withholding something from us. And we need to remember two things: as sinners, we don't deserve anything. Any and every material benefit in the here-and-now is due to God's free grace. Second, all (I mean, *all*) material blessing is a gift from God. It has no other source. In a truly Christian theology, it cannot have any other source: "Every good and perfect gift is from above, coming down from the Father of the heavenly lights" (James 1:17). You might think that the free market is the source of wealth; but who is it that created the mechanisms of the free market? To whom is Adam Smith's famous "invisible hand" attached? Note again God's warning in Deuteronomy: "You may say to yourself, 'My power and the strength of my hands have produced this wealth for me.' But remember the LORD your God, for *it is he who gives you the ability to produce wealth*" (8:17-18). The "invisible hand" is simply the Holy Spirit.

This leads to what I believe is the most foundational thing in a biblical view of economics: God is the source of prosperity and wealth, and this includes the structures and principles involved in obtaining prosperity and wealth. This may seem very basic, but consider some ways Christians unwittingly deny it.

GOD SUPPLIES SPIRITUAL AND MATERIAL BLESSINGS

When many people read of material blessings in the Bible, things like a "land flowing with milk and honey," or the upright man having "wealth and riches in his house" (Psalm 112:3), they have a very bad, reflexive habit of completely spiritualizing these things. God doesn't really mean wealth and riches. He means "wealth" and "riches," which are simply ciphers or analogies that really mean something like "spiritual well-being." Now, I believe that spiritual well-being is implied. I think these terms are analogies. That is why materially poor people who are loved by God can really, truly be called rich, and why fabulously wealthy wicked people are actually very poor. There are realities that transcend material wealth. But when wealth is understood to mean *only* spiritual wealth, it follows that God is only the source of *spiritual wealth*. But then we need to explain the source of actual, material, physical wealth! How do we explain all of this excess? It must come from someone or something else. Whom or what would that be? Completely spiritualizing the Bible's teaching on prosperity makes God the ultimate miser: not only is he stingy, but he doesn't give material blessings at all. This common mistake falls into the trap of making "stuff" the problem. God wouldn't soil his hands with dirty things like... money, would he? Well, yes, anybody who bothers to read the Proverbs would find that he actually cares about it a great deal.

Sometimes people do not completely spiritualize material prosperity, but they greatly downplay it or disparage it as unimportant. And this is understandable and, rightly qualified, correct. This recognizes that there are things of greater and lesser importance in the world. And it is clear that material wealth is not of ultimate importance: "What good is it for a man to gain the whole world, yet forfeit his soul" (Mark 8:36)? But there is a very big difference between being less important and being unimportant. This is a distinction Jesus understood, but one that his followers sometimes have difficulty with. Telling his followers not to worry about food, shelter, and clothing, he does not conclude that they do not need them. He says that his Father will take care of them and provide for them: "So do not worry, saying 'What shall we eat?' or 'What shall we drink?' or 'What shall we wear?' For the pagans run after these things, and your heavenly Father knows that you need them. But seek first his kingdom and his righteousness, and all these things will be given to you as well" (Matthew 6:31-33). This last phrase banishes forever the false dichotomy: the kingdom of God or material well-being. Jesus says, "as well." The same Jesus who forgave the paralytic his sins (and thus provoking the Pharisees) also *healed* him (Mark 2:1-12). The same should be noticed regarding all the people Jesus healed. Less important (physical healing versus forgiveness of sins) is not unimportant.

An example of people who have difficulty with this principle are those I call material minimalists. The idea is that God only wants people to have the bare necessities for life, the minimum, and that anything more than that is wasteful excess, especially if this excess happens at the same time that somebody somewhere does not have the bare necessities. This would include, for example, influential evangelical Ron Sider, author of *Rich Christians in an Age of Hunger: Moving From Affluence to Generosity*,[5] (Note: why is it affluence to generosity, as if they are mutually exclusive?) as well as Craig Blomberg, author of *Neither Poverty Nor Riches: A Biblical Theology of Material Possessions*.[6] In this view God is, pretty explicitly, a miser. The God who originally made a lavish Garden has definitely changed his spending habits. But when Jesus encouraged his followers not to worry, he pointed to the lilies of the field, and the essential point of the analogy is that "not even Solomon in all his splendor was dressed like one of these" (Matthew 6:29). In other words, God had lavished splendor on the *grass*. How much more will he give to people made in his image? God is pleased to give above and beyond the bare necessities. That is exactly what made Adam and Eve's original sin so absurd! There they were, in a fruitful garden, supplied with far more than they needed. The sin was not just wanting more; an important aspect of the sin was to want more when they already had everything.

But what about the Lord's Prayer, which asks: "Give us today our daily bread" (Matthew 6:11)? Doesn't that indicate that we should not desire anything above and beyond our basic, daily needs? By no means! By using the most minimal, mundane example possible, "daily bread," Jesus is indicating that God is the source of even the smallest material blessing. It is easy to view winning the Powerball lottery as an act of God. Look at the odds! It is a bit more difficult to see your coffee and toast that way. Jesus is training his disciples to see everything as God's care and blessing. He is not setting an upper limit on what we may desire or ask of God. Subsistence living is not the maximum allowable lifestyle, much less a biblical ideal.

Do not misunderstand me: desiring neither riches nor poverty (to quote Blomberg's book title) is not at all a shameful thing. It is taught right there in the Proverbs: "Keep falsehood and lies far from me; give me neither poverty nor riches, but give me only my daily bread" (Proverbs 30:8). But this prayer is followed by a rationale: "Otherwise, I may have too much and disown you and say, 'Who is the LORD?' Or I may become poor and steal, and so dishonor the name of my God" (Proverbs 30:9). The writer of this proverb recognizes that both wealth and poverty come with their own particular temptations. This is an Old Testament version of Jesus' instruction to pray, "Lead me not into temptation." It is, writes John Schneider, "reminiscent of Solomon's prayer for wisdom rather than great riches, expressing the proper humility humans should have before a God who really owes them nothing."[7] This prayer recognizes that poverty is not somehow immune from the same temptations as wealth: covetousness, envy, jealousy, bitterness, and greed are not the sole possessions of Wall Street fat cats. We saw plenty of that among the "Occupy" movements dedicated to destroying Wall Street! The general principle of the proverb is certainly true: too much can generate a forgetfulness of God (as Deuteronomy taught) and too little can generate envy and greed. But once we have accepted and internalized the general principle we are faced with the problem of defining "too much" and "too little." And that analysis is not a simple, one-size-fits-all sort of equation.

The idea that God only desires the bare necessities for people is a powerful one for people who want to shame and guilt-manipulate wealthy people. Again, run this thought experiment: If God only provides the bare necessities, from whom does wealth and prosperity come? Not God! Material minimalism denies that God is the source of wealth and prosperity and, once again, falls into the trap of making the "stuff" the problem. Since prosperity does not come from God, it must be suspect. It must come from some ungodly source: making a deal with the Devil, exploitation of others, or ill-gotten gain. This is extremely deficient theology.

Material minimalism is common, and comes in a variety of shapes and sizes. But in the final analysis it is extremely dishonoring to God. What parent gives their children only the bare necessities? Do they not delight in going above and beyond, exceeding expectations, being extravagantly generous? In this we are not superior to God: "If you, then, though you are evil, know how to give good gifts to your children, how much more will your Father in heaven give good gifts to those who ask him!" (Matthew 7:11) Material minimalism views God's lavish generosity with contempt, something unworthy of him. And we are on very dangerous ground when we call God's blessing a curse; indeed, Jesus actually called it an "unforgivable sin" to attribute to the Devil God's work (Matthew 12:31-32). We should be wary of people whose first knee-jerk reaction to extravagance is grumbling and griping:

> But one of his disciples, Judas Iscariot, who was later to betray him, objected, 'Why wasn't this perfume sold and the money given to the poor? It was worth a year's wages.' [....]
>
> 'Leave her alone,' Jesus replied. (John 12:5-7)

An apt reply, applicable to covetous Wall Street Occupiers raging against the "1%" and evangelical guilt-manipulators alike.

If the source of wealth and prosperity is God, the giver of every good gift, then we have no warrant to automatically assume that wealth and prosperity is suspect. Is it possible for people to become rich wickedly? Of course! Jesus ran into a number of them, mostly Roman tax collectors. So moved by Jesus' generosity, Zaccheus bumped up his charitable giving and paid restitution on his ill-gotten gains, but nowhere do we find a blanket condemnation of wealth. Jesus himself used economic examples in his parables, and even condemned the person who hoards his wealth by not investing his money with bankers and accruing interest (Matthew 25:26-27)! The point is that in Scripture the crucial distinction is always the ethical one of righteous vs. unrighteous or wise vs. foolish, not the material one of rich vs. poor. One can be rich and wicked, as well as poor and righteous: "Better a little with righteousness than much gain with injustice" (Proverbs 16:8). But the ideal, the way God intended the world to be (but is now frustrated by the fall) is for righteousness and prosperity to coincide because *God loves prosperity*: "The reward for humility and fear of the LORD is riches and honor and life" (Proverbs 22:4).

One of the more popular genres of Christian literature these days is one that I believe often falls short of careful, biblical thinking in this regard.

This is the genre of bashing "materialism." I would not dream of denying that materialism is a problem in the Western world. As we saw in God's instructions to the Israelites in Deuteronomy, vast material wealth does bring about temptations to trust in and worship the "stuff." We live in an age of incredible material wealth and prosperity, and preachers on the lookout for something to criticize do not need to look far to find it. That said, railing against the "American Dream" does not take much work or imagination and many who undertake the task quickly devolve into the mistake of thinking the problem is wealth and prosperity.

Materialism is the idolatry of wealth and prosperity—making "the bottom line" a god to be served and pursued at the expense of everything else. In the case of the prosperity or "health-and-wealth" gospel, even religious devotion is made to serve the goal of riches ("I love God so that he will make me rich!"). But if materialism is the idolatry of money, it means that wealth and prosperity *are not in and of themselves symptoms of materialism.* There is no biblical reason whatsoever to presume that the husband and father who arises early to work a long day, devotes himself to his vocation, makes a lot of money, lives in a nice house, and buys nice things—lives, shall we say, the "American Dream"—is guilty of materialism. Yet this is a governing presumption held by many an evangelical preacher. No, the symptoms of materialism have to do with other things: does he sacrifice his relationships with his wife and children on the altar of work? Is he generous to others with his money? Does he give money to charitable causes? Is he ostentatious? Does he flaunt his wealth for status purposes? What we are looking for are the symptoms of greed; and mere success does not equal greed. This slippery equation is why I am generally unmoved by criticisms of the "American Dream." Some rail against it as complacent or not radical enough for followers of Jesus, revealing an ascetic mentality in which the material world is something that should be eclipsed in genuine spirituality. But once we reject the dualistic either/or of "Jesus vs. The American Dream" (as though one cannot love Jesus and desire a good job, disposable income, and a house in a cul-de-sac), the critique becomes pretty shallow. For example, in his book *Radical: Taking Back Your Faith From The American Dream*, David Platt ends his chapter called, "How Much is Enough?" (A question he does not even attempt to answer, incidentally) this way:

> You and I have a choice. We can stand with the starving or with the overfed. We can identify with poor Lazarus on his way to heaven or with the rich man on his way to hell. We can embrace Jesus while we give away our wealth, or we can walk away from Jesus while we hoard our wealth. Only time will tell what you and I choose to do with this blind spot of American Christianity in our day.[8]

Even though Platt continually insists that wealth is not the problem, he has a paradigm that boils down to only these options: overfed or starving, poor on the way to heaven or rich on the way to hell, giving or hoarding. I will surely join him in saying that there are ways of pursuing the American Dream that are idolatrous, but I find his dichotomies extremely unhelpful. Andrew Sandlin gets the balance far better:

> Our Lord concludes the parable [of the rich fool] by warning the one 'who lays up treasure for himself, and is not rich toward God' (v. 21). That is to say, when one makes wealth an end in itself, with no reference to God and his will and glory; when one hoards wealth *rather* than hoarding God; when man's chief end is not to glorify God and enjoy him forever, but to get wealth and enjoy it forever, he sins. He covets. He is greedy. This is a sin that is committed by both multibillionaires and welfare moms, by Wall Street executives and Wal-Mart greeters. Greed is no respecter of bank accounts. We sometimes hear the expression, 'obscenely wealthy,' of the person who owns (let's say) six homes, 25 sports cars, and castle on the French Riviera. But come to think of it, wouldn't it be nice if everybody in

the world had those things? If we answer yes, we're acknowledging that it's not the wealth that we consider obscene, but something else. Maybe that something else is greed, but if so, it certainly can't be limited to wealthy people. The unemployed high school dropout who survives by forging welfare checks is greedy, perhaps greedier than the multibillionaire on the French Riviera.[9]

Christians sometimes have a hard time having a positive view of money. It is sometimes viewed, at best, as a necessary evil. Many are the evangelical non-profits that are reluctant to charge money for their products and services, as though making money for their efforts is unseemly. The general view is that for something to be Christian, it must be free. I need to put this starkly, because it is high time evangelicalism abandoned this mentality: distaste for money does not come from the Bible. It comes from the pagan idea that the material world, money included, is inherently filthy and corrupt, rather than "very good" as God created it. I was reading a magazine article about a person who, under the influence of Eastern mysticism, had renounced money as evil and sought to live life as a sage and prophet in the midst of American materialism. An important event in his journey occurred when he worked at a women's shelter for five years. While he wanted to help people, he felt guilty about getting paid for it. Receiving wages devalued his charity. Now, sometimes that can happen—for instance, if the women's shelter required *needy women* to pay him his hourly wage. But it is far more likely that a fully-funded charitable organization (thank God for wealthy donors!) was paying him to help needy women. And I cannot see anything unseemly or uncharitable about that at all.

This knee-jerk impulse to attack wealth and prosperity has its roots in paganism, which devalues the material world. It might be counterintuitive, but this is confirmed in the New Testament. It is quite amazing that when the Apostle Paul wants to tell us how pagan rebellion against God manifests itself, the first thing that comes to his mind is probably not the first thing that comes to ours: "For although they knew God, they neither glorified him as God *nor gave thanks to him* [...]" (Romans 1:21). Thanks for what, exactly? Thanks for everything! Thanks for the big, wide material universe he made for human habitation! Thanks for summer evenings, rewarding jobs, a full refrigerator, the splendors of science and technology, a Filet Mignon grilled medium-rare paired with an Old Vine Zinfandel. Pagans enjoy these things, but cannot bring themselves to give thanks to God for them. The Christian spirit is, Paul teaches, to be the mirror opposite:

> Let the peace of Christ rule in your hearts, since as members of one body you were called to peace. *And be thankful.* Let the word of Christ dwell in you richly as you teach and admonish one another with all wisdom, and as you sing psalms, hymns and spiritual songs with *gratitude* in your hearts to God. And whatever you do, whether in word or deed, do it all in the name of the Lord Jesus, *giving thanks* to God the Father through him (Colossians 3:15-17).

Three times in three verses: be thankful. Christians should feel guilty about not loving others, guilty about worshiping money, guilty about neglecting our spouses and our children for the demands of a bigger piece of the pie, and guilty about not being generous with our wealth. But feeling guilty about Western prosperity, guilty about the paycheck, the bonus, the vacation, the big house, the nice car, the new iPad, the swimming pool, or the cul-de-sac is not pious and sanctified: it is stone's throw from full-fledged paganism, a lack of thankfulness to God, from whom all these blessings flow.

PRINCIPLES OF PROSPERITY

God invented wealth. He is in the prosperity business. He created the ground to be tilled and that in response it would produce economic fruitfulness. Just as we saw with the issues of life and sexuality, God created the world with built-in design features when it comes to work and prosperity. Creation provides non-negotiable principles for economic productivity, and we will explore them in more detail in the following two chapters. Among them are private property, free markets, and economic incentives. It is not incidental that these principles are foundations for the unprecedented explosion of economic prosperity in the Western world. This is because, contrary to the conventional wisdom that capitalism is the fruit of post-Reformation Protestantism (the legendary "Weber thesis") or secular Enlightenment philosophy, it was in fact created in the so-called "Dark Ages" by religious guys in monasteries. Seriously. If you are reading this on your Kindle, you can thank the guys singing Gregorian chants as well as Amazon.com. I recommend reading all about it in Rodney Stark's *The Victory of Reason: How Christianity Led to Freedom, Capitalism, and Western Success.*

Like the principles of life and sexuality, economic design is hard-wired. It is not a matter of software or social conditioning. All else being equal (e.g., no sugar daddies) laziness will produce poverty approximately one hundred percent of the time. And, all else being equal (no unforeseen disasters or mitigating circumstances) industriousness and frugality will result in economic prosperity. Promoting private property rights, ensuring free markets, and not stifling return on investment will result in prosperity because that is the design.

Progressivism, however, does not like the design. It insists that all this is a matter of software instead of hardware. Humanity can be reprogrammed to create a world without private property, a world where markets are not free but are rigged to produce equal results, and a world where returns on investment can be reallocated with impunity by the State for the greater good. The magic formulas of progressivism lead, predictably, to economic stagnation instead of prosperity.

---

1. Lactantius, *Divine Institutes*, Ch.16.

2. Plutarch, *Marcellus*, 17.4.

3. Robert L. Heinlein, *Time Enough For Love* (Ace, 1987).

4. John R. Schneider, *The Good of Affluence: Seeking God in a Culture of Wealth* (Grand Rapids: Eerdmans, 2002), 3.

5. Ronald J. Sider, *Rich Christians in an Age of Hunger: Moving From Affluence to Generosity* (Nashville: Thomas Nelson, 2005)

6. Craig L. Blomberg, *Neither Poverty Nor Riches: A Biblical Theology of Possessions* (Downers Grove: InterVarsity, 1999)

7. John Schneider, *The Good of Affluence*, 115.

8. David Platt, *Radical: Taking Back Your Faith From the American Dream* (Colorado Springs: Multnomah, 2010), 140.

9. P. Andrew Sandlin, "Greed, Biblically (Re-)Defined," *Gentle Torrents* (May 20, 2012) (http://pandrewsandlin.com/2012/05/20/greed-biblically-re-defined)

CHAPTER FIVE
ON PRIVATE PROPERTY

Daniel Suelo lives in a cave outside of Moab, Utah.[1] Born in 1961 as Daniel James Shellabarger, a decade ago he renounced wealth, gave away his last cent, and wandered into the hills. He doesn't believe in possessions. He owns nothing. He doesn't work. He doesn't make money. Money is evil: "When I lived with money, I was always lacking. Money represents lack. Money represents things in the past (debt) and things in the future (credit), but money never represents what is present."

Profound stuff.

Mr. Suelo is the latest in a long historical line of fringe ascetic pilgrims who renounce private property. What is interesting is that he claims Christianity as an inspiration. For him, the Sermon on the Mount demands his lifestyle: "Giving up possessions, living beyond credit and debt, freely giving and freely taking, forgiving all debts, owing nobody a thing, living and walking without guilt [...] grudge, or judgment." Of course, one finds little, if any, of those things in the Sermon on the Mount, but we can give him a pass on that—after all, the poor guy doesn't own a Bible.

He actually got his inspiration from the Eastern religions, Hinduism and Buddhism. After living for a time in a Buddhist monastery in Thailand, he wandered to India, where he joined company with an entire group of penniless ascetics, the "sadhus." Suelo wanted to be a sadhu, but decided that it was not challenging enough: "A true test of faith would be to return to one of the most materialistic, money-worshipping nations on earth and be a sadhu there. To be a vagabond in America, a bum, and make an art of it—the idea enchanted me." And so he did.

This brings it into proper focus. It is a fundamental feature of the "monistic" or "collectivist" religions like Hinduism and Buddhism (e.g., "all is one") that stuff is the basic problem. Material possessions are what cause greed and envy. If we could just overcome our attachment to things then we would be at peace with ourselves, each other, and the divine. We will be a "brotherhood of man / sharing all the world," as a nauseating song puts it. (I'm not sure which is more nauseating: the song or its popularity?) The messy material world needs to be transcended or overcome—a peaceful utopia can only be achieved if we get rid of money, or at least the inequality money represents. Daniel Suelo thinks he is channeling the spirit of Jesus.

He is channeling the spirit of Karl Marx.

This chapter is very simple, and can be summed up in an easily memorized sentence: *The Bible teaches the right of individual private property.* Material possessions, stuff, or things are not the roots of human dysfunction. Humanity's problem is an ethical one, not a material one. Utopia will not be achieved if the happy time arrives, as in John Lennon's fevered imagination, when there are "no possessions." That's what the ancient Gnostics thought and modern-day Gnostics like Daniel Suelo still think. It is what the Eastern religions think. It is what Karl Marx, Friedrich Engels, Vladimir Lenin, and Chairman Mao all thought. And it is what modern progressives think. What was "Occupy Wall Street" about, if not the eradication of private property, the rebellion of the "have-nots" (the so-called "99%") against the "haves" (the so-called "1%")? Everywhere this utopian vision is tried the result is dystopian squalor—as my friend Andrew Sandlin pithily puts it, "Every attempt to create heaven on earth in the end creates a living hell." Once again, this is because progressivism is contrary to the created design.

THE BIBLE & PRIVATE PROPERTY

"You shall not steal" (Exodus 20:15). A simple enough commandment, yet it contains an entire worldview. God, the Creator of heaven and earth and giver of this law, is a giver of a vast diversity of gifts. And those material gifts are *property*. Just in case you missed it the first time, God puts an exclamation point on it by repeating the concept in commandment number ten: "You shall not covet your neighbor's..." anything. It's almost creepy, like some psychic we just met has just told us our entire life history. God seems uncannily aware of our tendency to think of possessions as a problem. He is not surprised by John Lennon, the Dalai Lama, or Occupy Wall Street. So he took the time to actually inscribe it in stone with his own finger: That which is yours is *yours*, and that which is your neighbor's belongs to *your neighbor*. That house in the cul-de-sac, that SUV, that country club membership, that housecleaner? Theirs. Not yours. Your comic books and PEZ dispenser collection? Yours. Not theirs. Simple enough concept, yet it is utterly staggering how vast swaths of humanity have not managed to figure out that this arrangement is... well, good.

On the surface the general complaint can sound like a juvenile temper-tantrum: "It's not fair!" for some to have more than others. We can have the economic discussion at the level of mere class envy. But the issues are a bit deeper than that—the fact that God had to repeat himself ought to be a tip-off. The issue is ultimately theological. Spiritual monism—represented by the Eastern religions and ancient Gnosticism—has several basic features, among them are these three: 1) The material world is inherently corrupt and evil, and so material possessions, if they are necessary at all, are necessary evils. This is the opposite of God's declaration that everything was "very good" in Genesis. 2) The goal is to absorb the individual into the divine "oneness," the collective. This is the opposite of the most fundamental distinction of all revealed in the first verse of the Bible: "In the beginning God created..." God is distinct from his creation. 3) Distinctions and inequalities are illusions that are transcended in the spiritual realm (e.g., Nirvana). This is the opposite of God's own establishing of distinctions at the very creation of all things ("according to their kinds").

Political scientist Eric Voegelin was idiosyncratic when in 1959 he identified the various progressive mass movements of the 20th century (e.g., Fascism, Nazism, Marxism, Communism) as essentially revivals of the Gnostic religions of the 2nd century. But he was incredibly perceptive. For all of these movements have in common the goal of eradicating economic distinctions and inequalities (material possessions are inherently bad), as well as absorbing the individual into the larger divine (remember Hegel!) collective of the State. It is no wonder that progressivism's antipathy to private property contrasts so starkly with the worldview of the Bible. If progressive collectivism is not exactly the same thing as religious monism, as Voegelin believed, it is at least a kissing cousin.

Progressivism believes in a command-and-control economy in which the Almighty State is the giver of all good things rather than Almighty God. It does not believe in Adam Smith's "invisible hand" which, I argued, is simply the Holy Spirit dispensing prosperity as he sees fit; it believes in the visible, coercive, and iron-fisted hand of the bureaucratic, managerial State which dispenses all things equally. The collective State is the divine reality into which the individual must be absorbed—the goal is Nirvana in the here-and-now. And to achieve this goal money and wealth must be "spread around." Only when everybody shares everything equally will there be the Gnostic utopia. The "holy grail" of progressivism is, and always has been, the eradication of private property. Politicians trying to get elected in America cannot put it in this kind of Marxist idiom, so they soften it with rhetoric of compassion and fairness. That does not stop them, however, from demonizing economically successful people, businesses, or industries and constantly stoking class envy between the haves and have-nots. Remember how John Hinderaker noted that perhaps in our economic rhetoric we ought to bear in mind the biblical injunctions against coveting? Exactly.

I am suggesting that anyone who cares even a little about the worldview of the Bible and the Judeo-Christian tradition should have nothing whatsoever to do with this toxic mentality. Again, I know that progressive politicians couch their rhetoric in seemingly benign, reasonable terms. President Obama speaks of "spreading the wealth around" in compassionate and moral terms, as though it is simply about helping out one's neighbor or being our "brother's keeper." Vice President Joe Biden calls it an issue of "basic fairness." But against all of it stands four incredibly stubborn words: "You shall not steal." This is not an "obscure line" in Exodus that we can replace with the Sermon on the Mount, Obama-style. It is one of the most famous legal injunctions in the history of the world, and it is responsible for the incredible prosperity evident in the Western world. It means that individual private property is fundamentally God-ordained and legitimate. For evangelicals devoted to the Bible, there is no escaping this fact.

MONEY DOESN'T GROW ON TREES

Progressivism denies the most basic economic reality passed down through the generations, generally from well-to-do fathers to their broke sons: "Money doesn't grow on trees." It comes from somewhere. In progressivism's "magic formula," it comes from a giant ATM in the sky that dispenses trillions and trillions of dollars, and there does not seem to be an upper credit limit. Politicians studiously avoid facing the stupidity of this. In keeping with their view that the Almighty State is god, they have their own creation myth: the State produces wealth as God originally created the universe: *ex nihilo*, "from nothing." Money really does grow on trees, in this thinking.

Once again, the Bible sets up some quite different parameters for money and wealth. Most importantly, the world was created in such a way that wealth is inextricably tied *to labor and industry*. It is not "free" (bringing to mind another colloquial economic lesson: "There's no such thing as a free lunch"). Yes, God placed Adam and Eve in a luxurious garden, but they were instructed to tend that garden, to work it, and to rule over it. In theology this is generally called the "dominion mandate," and it represents a command and a promise. And this command and promise was not done away with at the Fall, but rather reasserted. God told them that the land would still yield its harvest, but that their labor in getting it to do so would be vastly increased. It would take the "sweat of the brow" to yield produce.

Thus, from the very beginning labor has been the engine that produces wealth. This is hard-wired in human nature. The connection between work and reward provides economic incentives. Because God continues to providentially govern and maintain his original creation—that is, because hard work still produces economic benefit—human beings can be assured that their labors are not in vain. This connection between work and economic reward is taught time and again by the man the Bible describes (besides Jesus) as the wisest person to ever live: King Solomon. In the Bible's collection of his proverbs, it is presented as rock-solid economic law that labor produces prosperity and laziness produces poverty. Now, as a genre, proverbs are necessarily hyperbolic. They present general truths as absolute truths. Solomon is not, to say the least, stupid. He knew full well that some people have ill-gotten gains and that some people are poor for reasons other than laziness. But these are exceptions to the rule.

And this is, in fact, a rule. There are few people in the Bible as compassionate as the Apostle Paul. In his missionary endeavors he urged the churches in the Mediterranean world to contribute their money for the poor in Jerusalem. And yet, writing to the church in Thessalonica, he included these rather strict words:

> In the name of the Lord Jesus Christ, we command you, brothers, to keep away from every brother who is idle and does not live according to the teaching you received from us. For you yourselves know how you ought to follow our example. We were not idle when we were with you, nor did we eat anyone's food without paying for it. On the contrary, we worked night and day, laboring and toiling so that we would not be a burden to any of you. We did this, not because we do not have the right to such help, but in order to make ourselves a model for you to follow. For even when we were with you, we gave you this rule: 'If a man will not work, he shall not eat.' (2 Thessalonians 3:6-10)

Christian teaching upholds and maintains the creational mandate connecting labor and reward. It is not a Christian "suggestion." Paul calls it a command and a rule. If an able-bodied person will not labor, then that person is simply not entitled to the fruits of another's labor. For all the rhetoric used to justify redistribution of wealth (being "our brother's keeper," or "to whom much is given much is required") Paul seems to indicate that in some circumstances perhaps a job is better than a handout.

It is precisely this connection between labor and reward that is divorced in the progressive worldview. In the long tradition of socialism, the aim has always been wealth redistribution on an indiscriminate scale, regardless of the merits of the receiver. For example, when Representative Paul Ryan of Wisconsin suggested that perhaps Social Security payments ought to be "means-tested," meaning that only truly needy people should receive them (a blindingly commonsensical proposal), a progressive group literally created a television ad showing Representative Ryan pushing an elderly woman in a wheelchair off a cliff! Progressivism has built entire societies in which people are entitled to an income regardless of their actual economic contribution. It amounts to another broken (famous) rule of human nature: "Give a man a fish, feed him for a day; teach a man to fish, feed him for a lifetime." Progressivism is in the business of supplying free daily fish for everyone. You can see for yourself the results in modern European countries like France, Spain, and Greece. Whenever those governments cut entitlement programs in their various "austerity" programs, there is rioting in the streets. Europe is discovering, to their dismay, that there is not really a giant ATM in the sky—the money has to come from somewhere. It comes from people who work for a living. As Lady Margaret Thatcher put it in her timely wisdom: "The problem with socialism is that eventually you run out of other people's money."

By severing the connection between labor and wealth, work and reward, progressivism distorts basic creational economic reality. It completely distorts human nature—indeed, it does not believe in human nature. Like Marx, it wants to redesign human nature, to create a new "Socialist Man." Progressivism believes that it can forever confiscate the rewards of some people's labor and give it to others, blithely assuming that the economic victims will simply continue working without incentives. This is the rhetoric of policy gimmicks like Barack Obama's "Buffet Rule," which would entail a tax increase on wealthier Americans. (Never mind that "wealthy" is always a moving target.) The U.S. Government could confiscate all the collective wealth of the rich and still hardly put a dent in its financial obligations. And basic common sense (itself a built-in feature of creation) tells us what happens when we decrease the incentives for wealthy people to expand their wealth: they stop. If you only get to keep 20 cents on every dollar you earn, you will simply decide that the effort is not worth the reward. There is an ineradicable connection between work and reward. As the old adage has it, if you want less of something, tax it; if you want more of something, subsidize it. Raising taxes decreases economic prosperity and expanding (subsidizing) social welfare gets you more of it. Not only does progressivism ignore human nature by assuming that the wealthy will simply continue in their economic productivity without incentives, but it ignores human nature with respect to the recipients of this largesse. With their daily bread guaranteed by god (the State), they, too, lose all incentives to engage in labor and industry! This is why wealth-redistribution systems never produce prosperity. They undermine and depress the very thing that produces it: work.

The economic marketplace is not designed to provide equality of outcomes, where each and every person has an equal share of wealth, and the 8th and 10th Commandments make clear that this should not be a goal in the first place. The marketplace is designed to provide equality of opportunities. The civil government's job, as envisioned in the Bible, should be geared to rooting out dishonesty and deception in the economic markets. This is reflected in the Bible in Israel's laws: "Do not use dishonest standards when measuring length, weight, or quantity. Use honest scales and honest weights" (Leviticus 19:35). We all know what this means, because we see examples of it every time we fill our gas tanks. There is a sticker on every gas pump in America from the "Department of Weights and Measures" that certifies that this pump distributes exactly this much gasoline, no more and no less. This is an "honest weight and measure." This is clearly a legitimate government enterprise. What is completely beyond the government's business is making sure everybody has gasoline (or ethanol, electricity, or natural gas) in their vehicles. Everybody has the opportunity to buy this much gas at this price from this merchant; whether they actually do buy it is a matter of individual freedom of what to do with their own money.

MONEY & CAESAR

I have emphasized the absolute character of the law, "You shall not steal." Individual private property is assumed by a biblical worldview. But doesn't the government have the right to tax? Yes, the Bible teaches that, too. I am not saying that all taxes are stealing. I am saying that taxes can be stealing. There is a gigantic worldview difference between those two statements. Progressivism does not believe that taxation can ever rise to the level of stealing because it does not truly believe in private property at all. Property is the gift of the collective, a gift of the government, and what the State giveth, the State can take away. It is something of a fun parlor game played by conservative talking heads to ask their progressive counterparts on the nightly cable shows to define the terms "fair share."

How much is a "fair share" for the rich? There is never an answer because the progressive worldview does not allow the answer to be spoken out loud. There is, as a matter of principle, no upper limit.

Yes, Jesus tells his followers to "Give to Caesar what is Caesar's" (Mark 12:17). The civil government has a legitimate claim on some portion of a person's wealth. Paul tells the Roman Christians, "This is also why you pay taxes, for the authorities are God's servants, who give their full time to governing. Give everyone what you owe him: If you owe taxes, pay taxes; if revenue, then revenue; if respect, then respect; if honor, then honor" (Romans 13:6-7). It seems we now have a dilemma: the Bible teaches the right of individual private property, but doesn't give a clear limitation on how much the government can require individuals to give.

To resolve the dilemma, we must seek to understand what the Bible views as the government's role. We have already seen in the injunctions against false weights and measures that equality of wealth or equal outcomes in the economic marketplace are not areas for governmental intervention. It so happens that the Apostle Paul, in this very context, gives us guidance on the role of civil governments. He writes:

> [R]ulers hold no terror for those who do right, but for those who do wrong. Do you want to be free from fear of the one in authority? Then do what is right and he will commend you. For he is God's servant to do you good. But if you do wrong, be afraid, for he does not bear the sword for nothing. He is God's servant, an agent of wrath to bring punishment on the wrongdoer" (Romans 13:3-4).

Governments are instituted by God to do two general things: reward good behavior and punish bad behavior. Notice that what is in view is behavior. There is no hint here that the government should be rewarding or punishing for things other than the actions of its citizens. It should not be favoring some and disenfranchising others because of, say, socioeconomic status. It should not reward the poor simply because they are poor, or (as in the case of wealthy lobbyists and crony capitalism) rewarding the rich because they are rich. Favoritism based solely on economic status, in fact, is condemned by God! "[D]o not show partiality to the poor or favoritism to the great, but judge your neighbor fairly" (Leviticus 19:15). The basic, God-given role for the civil government is to reward and punish behavior, and redistribution of societal wealth (taxing the rich to give to the poor) simply does not fit this description. The basis of that kind of program is not behavior, but realigning things based purely on economic status. It inherently "shows favoritism."

Furthermore, the Bible gives other indications that the role of civil government should be limited. To point out the sometimes-forgotten obvious, the Bible everywhere condemns tyranny and oppression. The Exodus itself, the leading of God's people "out of the land of slavery," is a paradigm for what God envisions. Jesus defined his mission by appealing to a passage in Isaiah: "He has sent me to proclaim freedom for the prisoners and recovery of sight for the blind, to release the oppressed, to proclaim the year of the Lord's favor" (Luke 4:18-19). Freedom, release, liberty—this is the very heartbeat of God's plan. While the Bible teaches that the ultimate oppressors are sin and death, it certainly does not countenance lesser oppressors. And so the prophets are filled with denunciations of nation-states that oppress their people.

The Bible is incredibly realistic in recognizing the temptations of governmental power. Moses foresaw that the Israelites would one day desire to have a King rule over them, so he commanded that the King "must not acquire great numbers of horses for himself or make the people return to Egypt to get more of them [....] He must not take many wives, or his heart will be led astray. He must not accumulate large amounts of silver and gold" (Deuteronomy 17:16-17). When the day finally came for Israel to choose a King, the prophet Samuel put it even more starkly:

> This is what the king who will reign over you will do: He will take your sons and make them serve with his chariots and horses, and they will run in front of his chariots. Some he will assign to be commanders of thousands and commanders of fifties, and others to plow his ground and reap his harvest, and still others to make weapons of war and equipment for his chariots. He will take your daughters to be perfumers and cooks and bakers. He will take the best of your fields and vineyards and olive groves and give them to his attendants. He will take a tenth of your grain and of your vintage and give it to his officials and attendants. Your menservants and maidservants and the best of your cattle and donkeys he will take for his own use. He will take a tenth of your flocks, and you yourselves will become his slaves (1 Samuel 8:11-17).

In Samuel's mind, a civil ruler who takes but a tenth of people's property is equivalent to *making them his slaves*. This emphasis on "tenth" is incredibly significant because the Israelites were already required to give a tenth of their income to God. Samuel is warning that the state has the power to compete with God himself. Requiring a tenth is tantamount to Hegel's divinizing of the State. We are, sadly, a long way from Samuel's recommended 9.99% tax rate (maybe Herman Cain was on to something with his 9-9-9 plan!). But we can infer another principle from Samuel's warning: the biblical ideal is for the citizen-state relationship to be one of vast individual freedom and limits to what the King can require. He clearly believes that smaller government is preferable to bigger government. Returning again to Paul, civil government is "God's servant." Citizens are not servants of the state; it is precisely the opposite. The state is a servant, "God's minister" (literally: "Deacon") for the benefit of its citizens.

And biblical history records examples of how this principle is abused by rulers. When King Rehoboam took Solomon's throne, the people of Israel implored him to lower the high tax burden his father had imposed. Disregarding the wise counsel of his cabinet, he foolishly responded: "My father laid on you a heavy yoke; I will make it even heavier. My father scourged you with whips; I will scourge you with scorpions" (1 Kings 12:11). The King "did not listen to the people," (v.15), and the result was revolt. The Israelites even stoned to death Rehoboam's forced-labor "czar" (v.18)! One of the most famous examples of tyrannical overreach is the story of King Ahab and Queen Jezebel. They wanted a certain vineyard owned by Naboth the Jezreelite. Naboth refused to sell it to them (apparently the Kelo precedent hadn't been set and so "eminent domain" was not an option) so they framed him for treason, had him stoned to death, and took possession of the vineyard. Ahab and Jezebel were famous for their wickedness, but it was this event that provoked God to strike them down (1 Kings 21).

To summarize, then, the Bible everywhere condemns tyranny and oppression, describes the civil government's role as servant, places limitations on its powers, warns of excessive taxation, and warns the state not to divinize itself by assuming God's prerogatives.

CHRISTIAN COMMUNISM?

But some Christians on the leftward end of the political spectrum insist that the Bible teaches socialism and the redistribution of wealth. They generally point to three things to justify this claim. First, they simply point to all the injunctions in the Bible to care for the poor and oppressed. Second, they point to a concept in Israel's laws called the "Jubilee" year, where certain debts are cancelled and property returned to its previous owners. Third, they point to the early church as described in Acts chapter 2. Let us briefly explore these three lines of argument.

The first need not take much time, for it is essentially irrelevant. Obviously, God cares for the poor and oppressed, and in keeping with the second great commandment to "love your neighbor as yourselves" he commands people to be generous and to care for the poor. Nowhere in the Bible—and I do mean nowhere—is it suggested that the poor should be given money extracted by the government from wealthy people through taxation. In fact, as we will see in the next chapter, the reality is far from it.

The second line of argument involves an event peculiar in Israelite law: the Jubilee year. Every seven years the Israelites were required to cancel debts (Deuteronomy 15), and every fifty years there was a Jubilee where not only debts were canceled, but property is returned to its ancestral boundaries (Leviticus 25:8-55). This is, it is argued, a giant redistribution of land and wealth that justifies the concept of wealth redistribution by modern states. But let us note a few problems with this analysis:

1. All these requirements involve only Israelites. Debt cancelation did not apply to foreigners (Deuteronomy 15:3). It was an intra-family affair among God's people. It is presumptuous, therefore, to assume that these are universally-binding moral principles involving peoples and nations generally.

2. This was not, in any way, shape, or form, equivalent to indiscriminate property redistribution. Land was not given to just anybody who happened to need it, much less taken from the rich and given to the poor; rather, it was returned to its previous owners irrespective of their socioeconomic status. In some cases, no doubt, the land is

being transferred from poorer people to richer ones! Private property rights (intergenerational ancestral lands) are being wholeheartedly affirmed in the Jubilee law, not weakened. (By the way, we should note the irony that many Christian progressives appeal to the Jubilee law but support estate taxes that *liquidate* intergenerational property.)

3. The land to be returned in the Jubilee year was strictly agricultural property (Leviticus 25:15). God specifically made urban property immune to this law: a house in a "walled city" "is not to be returned in the Jubilee" (Leviticus 25:30). What we actually have, then, are not property sales, but fifty-year property leases for the purpose of agriculture. The Jubilee specifies that farmlands can be leased for a maximum of fifty years, at which time the land is returned to its previous owners. The law even says of a seller: "what he is really selling you is the number of crops," not the land (Leviticus 25:16). Also of note is that the person who has rented the land is not required to "redistribute" the income he made off of the property in the intervening fifty years.

4. The Jubilee law is not designed to eradicate the problem of poverty. In the very midst of the law we find exhortations about what to do when "one of your countrymen" becomes poor. You are to help him, loan him money without interest, so that "he can continue to live among you" (Leviticus 25:35-38). There would be no need for this exhortation if the Jubilee law itself was designed for the purpose of alleviating poverty.

Closer examination of the Jubilee laws shows that it is a gigantic leap from this Israelite practice to the modern idea of taxing the wealthy to redistribute it to the poor. In fact, there is nothing in the Jubilee laws that could possibly justify it.

The third line of argument for a kind of Christian socialism is found in Acts 2:44-45, where Luke records that "All the believers were together and had everything in common. Selling their possessions and goods, they gave to anyone as he had need." This appears at first glance to be a strong argument, but it really is not.

1. First, note the vast distance between an instance in which Christian believers share their property with each other and the notion of the government coercing people to hand over their money to be given to the poor. The one simply does not follow from the other.

2. We know that Paul and the other Apostles purposely set an example of not expecting entitlement or charity. "For you yourselves know how you ought to follow our example. We were not idle when we were with you, nor did we eat anyone's food without paying for it" (2 Thessalonians 3:7-8). So much for socialism.

3. As we will explore in the next chapter, charity is inherently not something that can be commanded or coerced. The Apostle Paul, writing about the generosity of the Macedonian churches, was amazed at their generosity: "Out of the most severe trial, their overflowing joy and their extreme poverty welled up in rich generosity. For I testify that they gave as much as they were able, and even beyond their ability. *Entirely on their own*, they urgently pleaded with us for the privilege of sharing in this service to the saints" (2 Corinthians 8:2-4, emphasis added). He goes on to exhort the Corinthians to do likewise, but explicitly writes: "I am not commanding you" (8:8). Why doesn't he command them? So that "it will be ready as a generous gift, *not as one grudgingly given*" (9:5). "Coerced charity" is a contradiction in terms; it might be a gift, but it will be a grudging one. Governments should learn this lesson.

4. Finally, we know that the outbreak of sharing in Acts 2 was not imposed on the believers. Acts 5 records a famous incident with Ananias and Sapphira, a wealthy couple in the Jerusalem church. They sold a piece of property in order to give the money to the church, but they held back a portion of it. Their sin was not that they held back a portion of it, but that they lied about it. Peter explicitly says to them, "Ananias, how is it that Satan has so filled your heart that you have lied to the Holy Spirit and have kept for yourself some of the money you received for the land? *Didn't it belong to you before it was sold?* And after it was sold, *wasn't the money at your disposal?*" (Acts 5:3-4, emphasis added). Peter positively endorses the fact that Ananias and Sapphira owned the property and had the right to dispose of the money after its sale. The sin was pretending to give it all to the church, but keeping some back.

Thus, the typical biblical rationales for softening individual property rights and endorsing State-coerced wealth redistribution are actually very, very weak.

CONCLUSION

The right of individual private property, free markets not rigged by the government to generate equal outcomes, and the creational relationship between labor and reward (economic incentives) are all affirmed by the Bible. It is one of the best-kept secrets that this combination of ideals, coupled with the broader Judeo-Christian worldview that material wealth or "stuff" is not problematic, is the basis of Western prosperity. One of the finest and most accessible treatments of how this is so can be found in a book mentioned previously: Rodney Stark, *The Victory of Reason: How Christianity Led to Freedom, Capitalism, and Western Success.*

But another book makes the case just as powerfully, and without any particular interest in identifying the specifically Christian roots of prosperity: Peruvian economist Hernando De Soto's *The Mystery of Capital: Why Capitalism Triumphs in the West and Fails Everywhere Else.*[2] The reason for Western prosperity and financial success is not found, as progressivism imagines, in colonialism or exploitation of third-world countries. It is found in something unique to the Western world: a system of formal, unified, legal property. De Soto and his team of researchers performed a vast experiment. They went through the process of trying to buy property and/or start businesses in a variety of economically depressed countries. They found a number of obstacles, all centering around the fact that these countries did not have an orderly and unified system of private property rights. Without clear individual private property, homes, lands, and businesses are unable to be capitalized. They are essentially "dead capital." De Soto discovered that third-world countries are not poor at all. They are sitting on vast mountains of wealth; but it is wealth that cannot be actualized or put to work because its ownership is ambiguous. If these countries were to adopt the Western practice of having a unified, formal system of legal property they would begin to experience something like the economic prosperity enjoyed in the West.

And I want to identify more specifically what that "Western" practice is: the Judeo-Christian ethic derived precisely from those stubborn four words, "You shall not steal." People are entitled to own property without interference. That principle has produced prosperity unprecedented in human history, and this simply cannot be denied.[3] What also cannot be denied is that this principle is fundamentally undermined by progressivism's perennial imagination of a utopian "brotherhood of man" where there are "no possessions."

1. Christopher Ketcham, "Meet the Man Who Lives on Zero Dollars," *Details*, (http://www.details.com/culture-trends/career-and-money/200907/meet-the-man-who-lives-on-zero-dollars?currentPage=1)

2. Hernando De Soto, *The Mystery of Capital: Why Capitalism Triumphs in the West and Fails Everywhere Else* (NY: Basic Books, 2000)

3. For one of the most astonishing visual displays of how this is so, watch Hans Rosling's five-minute BBC presentation entitled, "200 Countries, 200 Years" (http://www.youtube.com/watch?v=jbkSRLYSojo)

CHAPTER SIX

ON HELPING THE POOR

In a campaign speech in late March of 2012 President Barack Obama described what he believed is the economic philosophy of the opposition party:

> You know, if you're out of work, can't find a job, tough luck; you're on your own. If you don't have healthcare, that's your problem; you're on your own. If you're born into poverty, lift yourself up out of your own—with your own bootstraps, even if you don't have boots; you're on your own.[1]

"Tough luck; you're on your own." This is a common caricature of those who believe in free markets and oppose wealth redistribution by way of higher taxes on the wealthy. Progressivism has always portrayed the free market capitalist system as a dog-eat-dog, red in tooth and claw, Darwinian worldview where the rich get richer by exploiting the poor, the strong preying on the weak. Right on cue, the President and his surrogates have now taken to calling the limited government view of the opposing party "social Darwinism." Of the Republican plans to cut taxes and spending, he said: "It is a Trojan horse disguised as deficit reduction plans. It is really an attempt to impose a radical vision on our country. It is thinly veiled social Darwinism. It is antithetical to our entire history as a land of opportunity."² Mr. Obama went on in his campaign speech to present himself as a contrast: "I am my brother's keeper. I am my sister's keeper." Unlike those cold, heartless, uncaring conservatives, Barack Obama is a man who shares the Bible's desire to help the less fortunate.

Almost everything about the way he draws this contrast is wrong.

The question is not and never has been about whether to help the poor. The question is simply one of how to help the poor. And this debate does not amount to petty partisan differences. This is a collision of worldviews. President Obama's imagination for what counts as helping people without a job, without healthcare, and mired in poverty is very limited. And it is limited by progressivism's idolatry of the State. His vision is impeded by Hegelian blinders. Progressives simply cannot conceive of any method of alleviating poverty that does not involve the direct involvement of a centralized, all-powerful Federal government. An alternative vision of a smaller Federal government and more individual liberty is a "thinly-veiled social Darwinism" in which the less-fortunate are simply "on their own." These are the options for the progressive mind: people are either orphans or they are wards of the State. There is no intervening option.

Samuel Gregg writes: "President Obama finds it hard to conceptualize the possibility that private communities and associations might often be better at helping our neighbor in need than governments. Instead, his instinct is to search immediately for a political state-focused solution."³ This myopic view is nowhere better captured than a recent project undertaken by Mr. Obama's reelection campaign: an online, animated slideshow introducing a character named "Julia." The slideshow follows

Julia throughout her life, showing "how President Obama's policies help one woman over her lifetime."⁴

The slides present: 1) Julia is a child, helped by the Federal Head Start program which prepares her to succeed in life. 2) Julia attends a good high school, thanks to the Federal Race to the Top program. 3) She attends college, thanks to the American Opportunity Tax Credit and Federal Pell grants. 4) Poor Julia unfortunately needs surgery while in college, but thankfully her parents' health insurance covers her thanks to Federal healthcare mandates that require insurance companies to cover her. 5) Julia enters the job market and is guaranteed equal pay thanks to the Federal Lilly Ledbetter Equal Pay Act. 6) Thankfully, Julia isn't required to pay back all of her student loans, thanks to the generosity of the Federal government's takeover of student loan programs. 7) Julia doesn't need to worry about having children while she's embarking on her career, because the Federal government requires her insurance companies to provide her all the free contraception and preventative care she needs. This allows her to "focus on her work rather than worry about her health" (i.e., pregnancy is an illness). 8) Julia finally decides to "get pregnant" (strange phrase—do people passively "get pregnant"?) All of her prenatal care is provided by "free" Federal programs. 9) Julia's son Zachary now benefits from the same educational opportunities like Head Start and Race to the Top that she received as a child. 10) Julia decides to start her own business, and she qualifies for a Federal loan to help her get started. 11) At age 65, Julia enrolls in Medicare, which pays for her preventative care and prescription drugs. 12) At her retirement, Julia receives Social Security, which allows her to live out her days comfortably.)

Is there anything missing in this cradle-to-grave entitlement system? At least a couple of things. First, conveniently omitted from the entire slideshow is any discussion of who pays for all of Julia's Federal benefits.

This is because the source is a mythical giant ATM in the sky. Just check out the economic well-being of European welfare states to see where this story ends: with a governmental "austerity" program and Julia sitting helplessly in jail for throwing a Molotov cocktail into the welfare office because they took away her benefits. Second, at every momentous turn in Julia's life, the only institution that stands between success and catastrophe is the State. No family, no husband (not even when she decides to "get pregnant"!), no community, no friends, no church, no volunteer organizations, not so much as a local billiard or dart league. Just the beneficent Federal government, supplying all of Julia's needs. There is, frankly, no better illustration of the totalitarian (i.e., holistic, "all of life") character of the modern progressive State than President Obama's "Life of Julia" slideshow.

THE BIBLE & POVERTY

The Bible is very clear that societies must care the poor, the weak, the helpless, and the less fortunate, and it is not necessary to prove the point chapter and verse. There is no question about whether to help the poor. "You're on your own" might fairly characterize the libertarianism of Ayn Rand, but it is not a biblical option. The question is how to help the poor. And the Bible is quite instructive when it comes to the methods and means.

The first thing the Bible teaches is that helping the poor must come from the heart—charity must be *charity*. God has compassion on the poor, and he expects people to "image" him by likewise having compassion. We already saw this in St. Paul's exhortation to the Corinthians. He refused to command them to give in order to "test the sincerity of [their] love" (2 Corinthians 8:8). Paul recognized that a "commanded gift" is no longer really a gift, but rather something "grudgingly given" (9:5).

A welfare system funded by government coercion simply bypasses this biblical principle wholesale. It divorces the gift from the giver altogether; the money, in fact, is not given at all: it is taken. Far from inspiring compassion and charity, it produces bitterness and resentment on both sides of the transaction. These attitudes are evident any time you hear a wealthier taxpayer griping about lazy "welfare moms," and is reciprocated when those same "welfare moms" turn around and gripe about the miserly attitudes of the wealthier taxpayer. The result, in other words, is greater social disintegration, not cohesion. Christians have sometimes failed to recognize that "coerced charity" is an oxymoron. In an outstanding essay exploring the historical roots of this phenomenon, particularly relating to Roman Catholicism, Paul Rahe writes:

> [T]he leaders of the American Catholic Church fell prey to a conceit that had long before ensnared a great many mainstream Protestants in the United States – the notion that public provision is somehow akin to charity—and so they fostered state paternalism and undermined what they professed to teach: that charity is an individual responsibility and that it is appropriate that the laity join together under the leadership of the Church to alleviate the suffering of the poor. In its place, they helped establish the Machiavellian principle that underpins modern liberalism—the notion that it is our Christian duty to confiscate other people's money and redistribute it.[5]

Charity that is coerced is no longer charity. It is a tax, begrudgingly given. Far from instilling an attitude that "I am my brother's keeper, I am my sister's keeper," as President Obama imagines it, the coerced redistribution of wealth yields the opposite sentiments of resentment and envy.

The second thing the Bible teaches about helping the poor is that the connection between labor and wealth is not to be set aside. Pure entitlement goes against the grain of a biblical model for reducing poverty. Again, Paul declared it as a rule among the churches that able-bodied, "idle" people were not entitled to charity (2 Thessalonians 3:10). This is a confirmation of the Old Testament legal system's design for charity. One of the ways the Israelites were to help the less fortunate in their agrarian society was encapsulated in this law: "When you reap the harvest of your land, do not reap to the very edges of your field or gather the gleanings of your harvest. Do not go over your vineyard a second time or pick up the grapes that have fallen. Leave them for the poor and the alien" (Leviticus 19:9-10). This is repeated again a few chapters later: "When you reap the harvest of your land, do not reap to the very edges of your field or gather the gleanings of your harvest. Leave them for the poor and the alien" (Leviticus 23:22).

These are instructive laws. The first thing to notice is that the poor were not entitled to the fruits of the harvest itself. Rather, what was available to the poor were literally the leftovers, the fringes of the field not harvested and whatever happened to fall to the ground during harvest. There is nothing here about setting aside a percentage of the actual fruits of the harvest for charity. Landowners were certainly free to do this and at least one man in the Bible is heralded as a hero for doing this *out of his own generosity*. Boaz instructed his harvesters to actively pull stalks out of the sheaves and leave them on the ground for one particular "alien," the Moabite woman named Ruth—the great-grandmother of King David (Ruth 2:16). Boaz modeled the generosity of God himself, but it is precisely the fact that it was not a legal requirement, not coerced, not a government regulation that made his actions generous and praiseworthy.

In other words, coerced charity destroys the concept of philanthropy (literally "love of humanity"). It is a great thing to voluntarily set up a scholarship fund, run a rescue mission, or open a children's hospital; it is no great thing at all to pay your taxes. We can see again how progressivism is dehumanizing; by inserting the impersonal, bureaucratic State between the giver and the recipient as the arbiter of social welfare, both are correspondingly deprived: the one is deprived of individual freedom and responsibility to provide true charity, and the other is deprived of genuine thankfulness (it is, after all, called an "entitlement"). The one is coercively deprived of the *fruits* of their labor, and the other is deprived of the dignity of *labor* involved in receiving the fruits. Since the dominion mandate connecting work and reward is an aspect of being the image of God—what it truly means to be human—dispensing with this principle is, in essence, dehumanizing.

This brings me to the second thing about this ancient method of alleviating poverty: it required labor. If the poor wanted to gather the "gleanings," the fruits left behind after harvest, they had to actually work hard to get them. This, too, is emphasized in Ruth's story. The text gives a glimpse of the kind of back-breaking work gleaning involved. Boaz's harvesters noticed how hard Ruth worked. Explaining to Boaz who the woman was, they reported: "She said, 'Please let me glean and gather among the sheaves behind the harvesters.' She went into the field and has worked steadily from morning till now, except for a short rest in the shelter" (Ruth 2:7). The reason biblical law required labor for charity is to maintain the creation mandate, which ties economic incentives to work. Again, pure entitlement to another's wealth without labor or effort divorces this important biblical connection. The wealthy lose all incentive to keep working if their labor is automatically extracted and given to somebody else, and the poor lose all incentive to work if their economic well-being is guaranteed regardless of work. Gleaning laws ensured that the poor would be taken care of, but in a way that does not divorce the biblical connection between work and wealth.

Clearly not everyone in need of charity is able to work. In that case, pure generosity is appropriate and pleasing to God. It uniquely reflects his own character, for the truth is that nobody is worthy of his generosity. No one can repay the Lord for his gifts. One of the most moving passages in the Old Testament is when King David seeks out a crippled man named Mephibosheth, the son of his friend Jonathan. This lineage gave Mephibosheth a claim to Israel's throne, since his grandfather was King Saul. Rather than follow the customary ancient Near Eastern practice of executing all such rivals, David summoned him and said: "Don't be afraid, for I will surely show you kindness for the sake of your father Jonathan. I will restore to you all the land that belonged to your grandfather Saul, and you will always eat at my table" (2 Samuel 9:7). Mephibosheth's reply is one that we should all have in the face of such generosity: "What is your servant, that you should notice a dead dog like me?" (9:8) David restores and blesses a cripple; sort of like how Jesus, David's descendant, restores all of us "cripples." Generosity is the very heart of God, and we are to image him in this regard.

The Bible makes a distinction between those who are "able-bodied" and those who are not, those who can glean a field and those who cannot. A biblical social welfare system should, likewise, seek to maintain the creational connection between work and reward as far as possible. This is why Paul sets the rule that "if a man will not work, he shall not eat" (2 Thessalonians 3:10). A handout might be appropriate, in some circumstances, but better is a job or means of producing economic value. Second, notice that Mephibosheth had the opposite of an entitlement mentality. Who am I, that you should notice a dead dog like me?" David's charity, personally given without force or coercion, was seen for what it really was: charity. When charity is a matter of law and entitlement, it is no longer charity. The tendency then becomes for its recipients to depend on it and feel entitled to it.

In other words (leaving aside for the moment that the progressive vision for a mandatory wealth redistribution program violates the 8th commandment protecting private property) State-coerced welfare destroys both the concept of charity and the connection between work and reward. The result is the loss of economic incentives for rich and poor alike, as well as widespread social disintegration, bitterness, resentment, and envy. This irony should not be glossed over: those who advocate this system do so in order to reduce the gap between rich and poor, but the costs for achieving this economic equality (still mythical, last I checked) is deeper division between the classes. Indeed, they cannot even advocate for this system without resorting to class-warfare rhetoric, stoking resentment from the have-nots against the haves. So much for promoting social unity!

Again, going against the created design does not bring fruitfulness, prosperity, and human flourishing. It brings the exact opposite. Simply examining the history of the welfare states birthed by progressivism more than adequately establishes this point. It is most evident in the purest command-and-control economies that dispense with the concept of private property altogether: communist societies. What could be more compassionate than holding everything in common? What greater example can be found of a society where the government requires being "your brother's keeper" than that of communism? One half-glance at the hell on earth known as North Korea should disabuse you of the notion that this idea leads to human prosperity.

AMERICA, LAND OF THE FREE (ASSOCIATIONS)

Progressivism inserts the central government in between the rich and poor as the arbiter of charity, which is therefore no longer charity. Money extracted by the Internal Revenue Service is not a gift. Completely absent from this vision are any *mediating* institutions, lesser organizations or associations of people and communities. Given the presuppositions of the Hegelian State, the only "collective" recognized is the State. Hence, without the paternal State poor "Julia" is bereft of the blessings of life. Ostensibly, as the slideshow has it, were it not for the Federal government Julia would have been an ignorant child unprepared for school, forced into a bad high school, and unable to afford college. If she hadn't died on the operating table in college, she would have been bankrupted by evil medical providers. She would have been unable to afford abortions and contraception, and she would have been burdened with pregnancy and her career would have languished. And so on. As I put it before, progressivism only knows of two possible conditions: orphan or ward of the State.

President Obama mentioned that alternatives to this Statist model are impositions of a "radical vision on this country" and are "antithetical to our entire history as a land of opportunity." I am gratified that he brought up the vision and history of this country, because they tell a very different story. One of the most unique things about the United States of America is its civic culture and history of free and voluntary associations. Charles Murray writes that an "unparalleled aspect of American community life has been vibrant civic engagement in solving local problems."[6] He quotes Tocqueville's observation that "Americans of all ages, all stations in life, and all types of dispositions are forever forming associations." A tapestry of local community organizations binds together American society. Tocqueville's observations go on:

There are not only commercial and industrial associations in which all take part, but others of a thousand different types—religious, moral, serious, futile, very general and very limited, immensely large and very minute. Americans combine to give fêtes, found seminaries, build churches, distribute books, and send missionaries to the antipodes. Hospitals, prisons, and schools take place in that way. Finally, if they want to proclaim a truth or propagate some feeling by the encouragement of a great example, they form an association. In every case, at the head of any new undertaking, where in France you would find the government or in England some territorial magnate, in the United States you are sure to find an association.[7]

This is a largely-forgotten aspect of American culture. There was a time when nobody would have even wondered whether the Federal government should solve local problems because local communities were fully capable of handling them. This is because local communities were really *communities*. Murray gives an eye-opening glimpse of a single slice of what that sort of America looked like:

Here, for example, is the roster of activities conducted by associations affiliated with 112 Protestant churches in Manhattan and the Bronx at the turn of the twentieth century: 48 industrial schools, 45 libraries or reading rooms, 44 sewing schools, 40 kindergartens, 29 small-sum savings banks and loan associations, 21 employment offices, 20 gymnasia and swimming pools, 8 medical dispensaries, 7 full-day nurseries, and 4 lodging houses. Those are just some of the Protestant churches in two boroughs of New York City, and it is not a complete list of the activities shown in the report. Try to imagine what the roster would look like if we added in the activities of the New York Catholic diocese, the Jewish charities, then the activities of a completely separate and extensive web of secular voluntary associations.[8]

That is a breathtaking list, and the point is simple: contrary to the suggestion that without the Federal government "you're on your own," the reality is that in a healthy, vibrant, robust society you are *anything but on your own*.

There are all kinds of organizations and free and voluntary associations that could serve to solve local social problems like poverty. The problem is that when the government, with its (seemingly) limitless resources, decided to monopolize many of the functions formerly performed by these civic organizations, the Leviathan simply displaced this vast web of local community-based solutions. And Alexis de Tocqueville warned of this very thing: "The morals and intelligence of a democratic people would be in as much danger as its commerce and industry if ever a government wholly usurped the place of free associations."[9]

So the choice is not between "ward of the State" or "orphan." The choice is between coercion and freedom. This chapter could continue for many, many pages arguing that local, personal, and community-based is better than centralized, bureaucratic, and impersonal when it comes to actually helping the "least of these" among us. That is certainly true, I would argue—although others do so better—but my point is not merely a utilitarian one of "what works."[10] My point is that charity reconstituted as government-coerced social welfare inherently violates the worldview of the Bible. The Bible requires that charity be free and uncompelled in order to be true charity. Forcing charity is fundamentally dehumanizing because it robs the individual of his or her freedoms and responsibilities (not to mention property). And it is dehumanizing because it robs the recipient of the individual dignity involved in work and labor. It takes a heart-driven, personal investment into the lives of the less-fortunate and turns it into a sterile, impersonal financial transaction. This is the opposite of being "my brother's keeper." When charity is really charity, when it is mediated by local voluntary and free associations, compassion is strengthened, gratitude is fostered, relationships are formed, and dignity is upheld—in a word: it is *humane*. Rather than bringing people together and forming strong community bonds, the impersonal character of a progressive, State-driven social welfare model actually exacerbates class divisions, resentment, and envy. It tears communities apart, forever segregating and alienating rich and poor. It is enough to make one wonder what "community organizing" actually entailed for up-and-coming Chicago politicians.

Historically America has been a place unique in the world for the way its people, in free and voluntary community associations, helped those who needed assistance. The "safety net" was not provided by an agency far, far away, but by friends and neighbors, churches and charities. Progressivism's Hegelian idolatry of the State has persistently eroded that civic fiber, from the New Deal to the Great Society, to the point where its advocates simply cannot conceive of any other arrangement. Indeed, they call alternatives "thinly-veiled social Darwinism." That phrase helpfully amplifies my point that progressivism is dehumanizing: in their worldview, without the oversight of the Almighty State people will devour each other like animals. That is its real assessment of human beings. All the talk about the divinity and goodness of man is, we must presume, strictly a future to be realized in the coming utopia. For now, unless people are forced to help each other by the coercive State, they will simply say to each other: "You're on your own."

The Bible, too, has a dim assessment of humanity—we are "fallen" sinners. But that does not make us animals. We still bear the image and likeness of God (James 3:9). God has not left us to our own devices. In his providential grace, he intervenes precisely to keep us from becoming nihilistic, Darwinian animals. Jesus says that even evil people "know how to give good gifts" (Matthew 7:11). In the progressive worldview, the State once again takes on a divine prerogative: rather than trusting God's grace to uphold social cohesion and motivate generosity, the State must force us to be kind to one another. And that kind of coercion is antithetical to liberty and freedom. We should not simply desire a virtuous society; we should desire a *free* and virtuous society. Indeed, without that freedom, virtue (being "my brother's keeper") is no longer virtue—it is an obligatory duty "grudgingly given."[11]

---

1.   "Obama blasts GOP's 'you're on your own' economics," *Los Angeles Times*, March 30, 2012 (http://articles.latimes.com/2012/mar/30/news/la-pn-obama-vermont-campaign-20120330

2.   Chris McGreal, "Obama accuses Republicans of 'social Darwinism' over Paul Ryan budget," *The Guardian*, April 3, 2012 (http://www.guardian.co.uk/world/2012/apr/03/obama-accuses-republicans-social-darwinism-budget)

3.   Samuel Gregg, "So who is our keeper, Mr. President?" *Acton Commentary* (May 16, 2012) (http://www.acton.org/pub/commentary/2012/05/16/so-who-our-keeper-mr-president)

4.   (http://www.barackobama.com/life-of-julia)

5.   Paul Rahe, "American Catholicism's Pact With the Devil," *Ricochet* (February 10, 2012) (http://ricochet.com/main-feed/American-Catholicism-s-Pact-With-the-Devil)

6.   Charles Murray, *Coming Apart*, 238.

7.   Charles Murray, *Coming Apart*, 238-9. Emphasis added.

8.   Charles Murray, *Coming Apart*, 239.

9.   Gregg, "So who is our keeper," *Acton Commentary*

10. I would recommend in this regard the work of the Acton Institute (http://www.acton.org) and The Heritage Foundation (http://www.heritage.org/issues/poverty-and-inequality); see also Steve Corbett & Brian Fikkert, *When Helping Hurts: How to Alleviate Poverty Without Hurting the Poor...and Yourself* (Chicago: Moody, 2009)

11. C.f., Robert A. Sirico, *Defending the Free Market: The Moral Case for a Free Economy* (Washington: Regnery, 2012)

PART THREE

JUSTICE

CHAPTER SEVEN

GOD LOVES JUSTICE

Justice is a very popular word in contemporary American culture. But simply because something is popular doesn't mean it is understood. Terms like "economic justice" or "social justice" or "racial justice" or "environmental justice" are vague and ill-defined, not because we do not understand words like "economic," "social," "racial," or "environmental," but because we do not understand what is meant by *justice*.

The classic image of justice in western civilization is embodied in the statue that stands outside the United States Supreme Court in Washington, D.C. It is a lady, standing tall, with scales in her hand. The most important feature of the image is that she stands blindfolded. Justice is blind. She is not a respecter of persons. Her judgments are not swayed by money, power, or influence. Each and every person who stands before her stands equally. We will see in this section that progressivism fundamentally alters this picture by *removing the blindfold*. Rather than holding each and every person to an inalterable, common, universal standard of behavior, under the new magic formula a person is rewarded precisely because of one's status. Lady Justice plays favorites. She metes out rewards and punishments based on whether one belongs to this minority group or that economic class, this racial group or that sexual orientation. The new formula for justice is the exact opposite of what justice really is.

We saw clearly in our first two sections that a Christian understanding of creation is crucial for understanding the dignity of human life and the mechanisms of prosperity. Creation is no less important for understanding the concept of justice. And it is important to notice that in each of these areas it is not really creation that is crucial, but rather the Creator. In the final analysis people, prosperity, and justice are important because of who God is. Human life is precious because it is the image of God himself, a creaturely "copy." It is God who endows human beings with dignity; we are important because of the one whose image we are. Prosperity is important and possible because, first and foremost, it is God who delights in abundance. And, as we will see in this section, justice finds its source and significance in the character of God.

Evangelical theology insists that not only is this an ordered universe that resists efforts at re-wiring, it is a *morally* ordered universe. That is because, first and foremost, God is just. God himself, his very own character, is the moral standard that stands in judgment of human beings. This is encapsulated in his exhortation to the Israelites to "be holy, as I, the LORD your God, am holy" (Leviticus 19:2). This is glossed by Jesus as, "Be perfect, therefore, as your heavenly Father is perfect" (Matthew 5:48). Like father, like children. Like Creator, like creature. If you think about it, there could be no higher moral standard or authority for human behavior. If God really is the Creator of all things, having literally spoken it all into existence, then there is no higher authority to whom we have to answer.

Thus, Christian theology teaches that there is a transcendent standard of morality and justice. That simply means that it stands above the ebb and flow of history. What is good, right, and true is always good, right, and true, no matter the historical situation. It means that we, as creatures, do not invent or make up the good, the right, and the true. It is our duty to submit to the good, right, and true. Just as we do not make the world but encounter it, so also we do not make up the rules of morality, we encounter them. That also means, no matter how much we might wish it to be otherwise, the standards of justice are inflexible. This is inherent to the very idea of justice, and is why the Bible contains strong condemnations for perverting justice (Exodus 23:6; Deuteronomy 16:19; 24:17; 27:19). To alter, morph, or tweak the standards to achieve a desired outcome is the very definition of perverting justice.

It is precisely the idea of a transcendent law above earthly laws that gave birth to Western liberty. The *Magna Carta* (A.D. 1215), one of the great revolutionary documents of liberty, expressly placed the King himself under a higher authority. Without this concept of a higher authority, there could have never been the legacy of British common law, with its protections of, say, the right to property, because kings and tyrants can always refashion the rules whenever it benefits them. And it is to the concept of transcendent justice that the founders of America appealed in their Declaration of Independence: "the laws of nature and of nature's God." They understood that the morality and justice of their actions could not be grounded simply in the fact that they desired independence. They had to justify—give reasons for—their desired independence. So they appealed to a higher authority by which to make their claims; specifically, that God had created all men equal and endowed them with rights that are inalienable and cannot be stripped away: the right to life, liberty, and the pursuit of happiness.

GOD IS JUST

The Bible has much to say about justice, and the first thing to notice is that the standard is anything but arbitrary. It is defined by the character of God himself. Moses declared in a famous song (did you know Moses was a songwriter?), recorded in Deuteronomy 32:4:

> He is the Rock, his works are perfect, and all his ways are just. A faithful God who does no wrong, upright and just is he.

Likewise, the Psalmist praises God's attribute of justice:

> For the word of the LORD is right and true; he is faithful in all he does. The LORD loves righteousness and justice; the earth is full of his unfailing love. (Psalm 33:4-5)

Even a pagan king was brought to this conclusion:

> Now I, Nebuchadnezzar, praise and exalt and glorify the King of heaven, because everything he does is right and all his ways are just. (Daniel 4:37)

And the saints in the age-to-come will sing a re-mixed version of Moses' song:

> Great and marvelous are your deeds, Lord God Almighty. Just and true are your ways, King of the ages. (Revelation 15:3)

It would actually become tedious to rehearse all the instances where the Bible praises God's attributes of righteousness and justice. God is obviously just. More important to our purposes is the fact that God's righteousness and justice form the standard to which human beings ought to conform. Psalm 11:7 says that "[T]he LORD is righteous, he loves justice; *upright* men will see his face." Human beings are, remember, God's image-bearers, creaturely models of God himself. God desires that those who bear his image would speak and act as he would speak and act. The very principle of bearing the image is this: like father, like children. A comparison of Proverbs 2:6-9 with Psalm 37:28-31 illustrates the principle.

> For the LORD gives wisdom, and from his mouth come knowledge and understanding. He holds victory in store for the upright, he is a shield to those whose walk is blameless, for he guards the course of the just and protects the way of his faithful ones. Then you will understand what is right and just and fair—every good path. (Proverbs 2:6-9)

> For the LORD loves the just and will not forsake his faithful ones [...] The mouth of the righteous man utters wisdom, and his tongue speaks what is just. The law of his God is in his heart; his feet do not slip. (Psalm 37:28-31)

The Proverbs passage emphasizes God as the teacher: from his mouth comes knowledge and understanding. The Lord "gives wisdom." The Psalm, using almost identical language, emphasizes people as the students: the mouth of the righteous man utters wisdom and justice. Where does this person learn the ways of God? How is one to know what righteousness and justice are? The Psalmist tells us: "The law of God is in his heart." God has not kept himself aloof, allowing us to grope about for how we should live: he has written it down, literally with his own finger: "When the LORD finished speaking to Moses on Mount Sinai, he gave him the two tablets of the Testimony, the tablets of stone inscribed by the finger of God." This is referring, of course, to the Ten Commandments, which serve as a summary of God's moral law.

THE LAW OF GOD IS JUST

Ah, yes. The Ten Commandments. They are the subject of seemingly endless litigation in an America today where it seems that a few cannot even stand the sight of them, much less obey them! One would think, given the antipathy expressed by atheists offended at their public display, that the Ten Commandments represent some fairly perverse ethical norms. It is time to stop hyperventilating about how wretched the world would look if they were implemented and to take another look.

The commandments are commonly understood to divide into two sections: the first four represent our duty to God, and the remainders express our duties to each other. This is why the Jews, Jesus included, understood that the law could be summarized as *loving* God (1 through 4) and *loving our neighbors* (6 through 10). In addition, it is commonly understood that these commandments are not simply negative duties ("Thou shalt not") but rather imply positive duties as well ("Thou shalt"). In other words, the 6th Commandment does not simply mean that I should not kill my neighbor; it means that I have a positive duty to protect my neighbor's life and to seek his or her welfare. It means (to cite one of my pet peeves) that I should move to the side of the road when an ambulance is barreling down the road. Somebody's life could be at stake! Moreover, as this indicates, each commandment is a summary command; "Thou shalt not murder" encompasses more than just that simple command. It stands for a whole host of duties regarding the protection of life, like getting out of the way of an ambulance. Or to use a biblical example, the ancient Israelites were required to provide barriers around their roofs, since they often entertained guests there. They understood the 6th Commandment to require reasonable protections against people falling off of the roof! I will have more to say in the following chapter about the first four commandments and our duties to God, particularly with respect to the propriety and possibility of enforcing them as law in a modern, pluralistic society.

But for now, just reflect on a few questions:

What if everyone took God seriously (#1 through 4)?

What if everyone honored, respected, and submitted to lawful authorities (#5)?

What if everyone always sought to protect the lives and welfare of their fellow human beings (#6)?

What if everyone were thoroughly committed to their own spouses, and sought to prevent sexual exploitation (#7)?

What if everyone refused to steal the property of others and affirmatively protected their material welfare (#8)?

What if everyone told the truth, and never sought to manipulate and frame others (#9)?

What if everyone were content with their own possessions, their own opportunities, and their own potential (#10)?

As difficult as it is to believe, these are the commandments that people really, seriously have issues with. And there seem to be two main reasons. First, there are people who really, truly want the freedom to rebel against all authority, murder others, be sexually promiscuous, steal property, lie and manipulate, and covet that which they do not have. I have a difficult time having sympathy for this class of objectors.

More frequently, opposition is based on the mantra that "you cannot legislate morality." And, since the Ten Commandments represent a distinctly religious moral code, it is inappropriate to legislate these things. The problem with this line of reasoning is not just that all legislation seeks to enforce some moral code (that is the whole point: declaring something to be *wrong*), but that we already do legislate the Ten Commandments! A great many of the most treasured laws in America have their basis precisely in this moral code.

For example, for all the insistence in our culture on sexual liberty, we legislate sexual morality quite heavily. And that is not because we are a nation of Victorian prudes. We have laws against all sorts of sexual crimes, the interest of which is to protect people from sexual exploitation—the very purpose of the 7th Commandment. We have child pornography laws and laws against the sex slave trade. We have laws against rape, child molestation, bigamy, polygamy, and bestiality. We have laws against prostitution. And until just a few years ago, we had laws against same-sex intercourse. And we can't legislate the 7th Commandment? Nitpick if you will about that list; Dan Savage is free to call some of it "bulls—t" from the Bible, but the fact remains that everyone believes that certain sexual behaviors are morally wrong. And God's law provides a solid foundation for believing exactly that. Dan Savage's foundation is whatever he personally happens to like or dislike.

But what about lying? It would be absurd to legislate the 9th Commandment, wouldn't it? Except that we actually do. "You shall not bear false witness," God says. And, sure enough, we have laws against perjury. And slander. And libel. And fraud. And insider trading. And obstruction of justice. Again, the 9th Commandment provides a solid moral foundation for these laws. Not only that, but in the development of all of these laws in the common law tradition we have inherited in America, explicit appeal was made to biblical law! A perusal of, say, Sir William Blackstone's *Commentaries on the Laws of England* (1765) will reveal just how strongly the Western legal system is dependent on distinctly biblical ethical foundations.

We could undertake the same exercise with the 6th and 8th Commandments, regarding murder and theft, respectively, but I trust there is no need. The fact that there is widespread agreement on many of these laws illustrates just how profoundly our culture has been influenced by the Christian tradition. The question is whether one can keep the legacy without the moral and intellectual tradition that provided the legacy? Can we destroy the foundation but keep the house? No sooner than the U.S. Supreme Court struck down a law against homosexual conduct (Lawrence v. Texas) on the basis of a "right" of sexual autonomy did the polygamists want in on the action. Remove the beams underneath the floor and the floor falls. It is very gratifying that this question is now being raised more and more in public conversation, even in places like *The New York Times*. Columnist Ross Douthat recently took on the question of the Christian foundations for the notions of human dignity and human rights, concluding in part:

> [My] whole point is that I don't think that many humanists actually do have strong reasons for their hopes regarding human dignity and human rights. I think that they have prejudices and assumptions and biases, *handed down as an inheritance from two millennia of Christian culture,* which retain a certain amount of force even though given purely materialistic premises about mankind and the universe they don't actually make much sense at all.[1]

NO TRANSCENDENT JUSTICE?

When justice is no longer transcendent, something universal, standing above the ebb and flow of history, then it must be identified with something in the ebb and flow of history. Unfortunately, there is only one other option. Justice is defined by the powerful. Whether the powerful is a single tyrant in the case of a monarchy or a bullying majority in the case of a democracy, justice is made to serve the desires and needs of human beings at a particular moment rather than human beings serving the desires and needs of justice at all moments. This is a fundamental transformation of the moral order of things, and its effects are truly perverse.

Friedrich Nietzsche understood this transformation, although he probably would not have agreed to its perversity: the "death of God" means that human beings must replace the transcendent moral order with an "immanent" moral order. We must become our own law, our own standard of justice. There is reason Nietzsche wrote a book called *Beyond Good and Evil*. Dostoevsky warned in The *Brothers Karamazov* that once God is dispensed with, "man will be lifted up with a spirit of divine Titanic pride and the man-god will appear."[2] This is precisely the worldview of Hegel and Nietzsche. So what replaces the moral order of a transcendent God? Again, there is only one option: the powerful decide. If there is no higher authority standing on the playground, no protective mothers or fathers keeping an eye on things, the bully gets to make the rules every single time. This is why Nietzsche spoke of the human ideal as the *Wille Zur Macht*, the "will to power." Unless there is a higher authority around, might really does make right, and only the powerful will thrive.

Denying the concept of a transcendent standard of justice is not only a recipe for tyranny, it is a recipe for all sorts of dangerous moral relativisms. What I am arguing here is not that atheists are all really horrible moral monsters. This is a point that the late Christopher Hitchens, the infamous atheist, couldn't (*no, wouldn't*) bring himself to face.[3] He routinely responded to this moral critique of atheism with the blindingly obvious observation that, yes, in fact, lots of atheists do really good and noteworthy deeds. That is decidedly not the point. The point is that the atheist has no sound, principled reason to adhere to a given moral code. People who have rejected transcendent justice might replace it with all sorts of strict moral codes (and they do: human beings cannot live without moral codes, after all) and they may even adhere to those codes. Certainly Christopher Hitchens had a finely-tuned moral sense when it came to the things he despised, such as murderous Islamic Jihadists and child-molesting Roman Catholic priests!

However, there remain two basic problems. First, the standards are not transcendent and therefore universally applicable. They are immanent, this-worldly standards, invented and, indeed, reinvented by people throughout history. There is no principled reason why one person's moral code is superior to anyone else's moral code. If we are all the descendants of pond scum, complicated amoebas floating in an ultimately meaningless universe, why should one product of the blind evolutionary process be privileged over some other, equally legitimate, product of the process? This is what is so baffling about the insistence of neo-atheists like Hitchens and Richard Dawkins that Christian ethics are *evil* (as in Hitchens's statement that Christianity is a "wicked cult" or Dawkins's book title, *The God Delusion*). On their own terms, Christian ethics are the outflow of a blind evolutionary process. As Douglas Wilson is fond of arguing, if you spill a glass of milk it doesn't occur to you to blame the milk. Yet evolution produced (for the sake of argument) billions of people who have a certain set of ethics based on Christianity. It makes no sense on those terms to blame them or call them evil and delusional. Without a standard of justice that transcends the world, the principle (not necessarily practice) of moral relativism is simply set in stone. The only way to negotiate our differences if all differences are equally legitimate is, again, raw power.

The second problem is that the purpose of moral codes is to provide a restraint on our behavior *when it is inconvenient*. R. R. Reno points out that Dostoevsky's warning that without God "everything is permitted" does not mean that without God each and every person will be as bad as they can be, as Hitchens imagined the argument to run. Rather, what it means is that "nothing is always wrong. Everything is, at least at some point and under some circumstances, permitted."[4] If human beings are self-legislators, then by definition moral standards are malleable and flexible. They are lumps of silly putty, to be fashioned as we wish. They must change to suit new circumstances. They must operate as pseudo-providence, engineering reality so that everything will work out for the good in the end. Reno perceptively writes:

> The language of human rights has become very influential in recent decades, suggesting that our secular world is capable of a new set of strong moral norms that can replace the old absolutes. Yet, without religious belief I doubt that the West can sustain a robust commitment to rigorous moral principles of any sort. Relativism has a moral mission. Its goal is to allow us to adjust to difficult situations, making exceptions to moral principles, or revising them to better fit human realities and mitigate human suffering. In dire circumstances what is normally prohibited is permitted. And as we get accustomed to our roles as moral commanders-in-chief the threshold gets steadily lower.[5]

In other words, if we deny a transcendent standard of justice, there is nothing to stop us (indeed, we are encouraged to!) from crafting our moral standards to suit our circumstances. Is this not the explicit rationale of progressive legal thinkers who advocate a "living" constitution, one suited to reflect our shifting morals? Instead of operating as a restraint on our behavior at inconvenient times, we simply shift our morality to alleviate the inconvenience. Surely I shouldn't have to bear this unwanted child? Surely I shouldn't be faithful to this cold, nagging spouse? Justice, the right thing to do, does not stand over us; we stand over justice, directing it to alleviate our ethical difficulties in "dire circumstances." And, as Reno rightly notes, "The progressive mentality tends to see dire circumstances everywhere." In this worldview, the desired results shape the standards of justice, rather than the other way around. Indeed, the desired results are outright confused with justice! Rather than the application of impartial principles to a given set of circumstances and letting the chips fall where they may, justice is making the chips fall a certain way.

President Obama gave voice to this novel understanding of justice when he nominated to the Supreme Court Sonia Sotomayor. In his nomination speech, he said that an outstanding intellect and recognition of the limits of the judicial role were not enough. A judge must have experience. Why experience? "It is experience that can give a person a common touch and a sense of compassion; an understanding of how the world works and how ordinary people live. And that is why it is a necessary ingredient in the kind of justice we need on the Supreme Court."[6] In other words, a judge with life experience will be able to have sympathy for one or more parties involved in a lawsuit. And, for her part, Ms. Sotomayor concurred, reiterating that her real-world experiences, her understanding of how her rulings would impact people (how the chips fall) would be a factor in her judicial analysis. This, in fact, had been a staple of her judicial worldview over her entire career. She was known in her speeches to include this line, repeatedly, word-for-word: "I would hope that a wise Latina woman with the richness of her experiences would, more often than not, reach a better conclusion."[7] So somehow, in some way, the outcome is better because of the race and experiences of the judge? This is a bizarre sentiment that only makes sense if it involves a view of justice that does, in fact, have the blindfold removed. The judge is to be sympathetic to one of the parties. In this case, unless she was literally saying that people of Latin descent are smarter than other racial groups (unlikely), the only reason the word "Latina" appears is to suggest she would have greater sympathy for minority groups in her rulings.

The Bible recognizes that the alternative to a fixed, transcendent standard of justice applicable to all is for the powerful to prey on the weak. There is a reason why it constantly exhorts people to do justice for the poor, for the widow, for the orphan, and for the oppressed. What do these classes of people have in common? In ancient times, they were the weakest members of society. God understands that when justice is defined by the powerful, they will tend to define it in such a way as to protect their interests at the expense of the weak. Deny a higher law, and tyranny is the result. This is why God commanded the kings of Israel to personally, by their own hands, copy the scroll of Deuteronomy and to keep it with them at all times and read it every day (Deuteronomy 17:18). Perhaps it is not a bad idea to require that all legislators and executives in government hand-copy the Constitution and read it every day!

Scripture also recognizes that tyranny is not simply the province of a single tyrant. There is such a thing as a tyranny of the majority. God instructs: "Do not follow the crowd in doing wrong. When you give testimony in a lawsuit, do not pervert justice by siding with the crowd" (Exodus 23:2). Several things are striking here. First, it clearly means that justice is something above and beyond cultural conventions. Cultural conventions are precisely *what crowds think*. A "crowd" is the court of public opinion, we might say, or majority rule. But according to the Bible the immorality of, say, murder does not rest on the fact that, well, "everybody knows..." It is very nice that many people (the crowd) agree on that point, but that is not what makes it wrong. The Bible here declares that majority rule is insufficient to establish whether something is just or not. The minority, the weak, need to be protected from the strong when they are perverting justice, and so God disapproves of witnesses and judges who automatically side with public opinion.

And yet I left out the rest of the verse, which adds something amazing: "and do not show favoritism to a poor man in his lawsuit."That a minority is a minority, or a poor person is poor does not entitle him or her to judicial favor! What God is clearly teaching is that status or identity is utterly irrelevant to the matter of justice. Rich or poor, popular or unpopular, majority or minority, black or white, slave or free, none of it is relevant to justice. "Do not pervert justice; do not show partiality to the poor or favoritism to the great, but judge your neighbor fairly" (Leviticus 19:15). Yet we live in a day and age when identity politics positively reigns. Who you are, your status or identity, is a very large ingredient taken into account in our law courts, to the point where a Supreme Court justice brags that being a "wise Latina" enables her to give better judicial outcomes! And that is the point: justice is not whether this or that person conforms to the standard of the law; it is whether the desired outcome, which could have any number of rationales, is achieved.

Once justice is confused with desired outcomes it is completely untethered to transcendent moral standards. It is completely arbitrary. One legal theorist describes the resulting basis for judicial analysis: "History or custom or social utility or some compelling sentiment of justice or sometimes perhaps a semi-intuitive apprehension of the pervading spirit of our law must come to the rescue of the anxious judge, and tell him where to go.[8] History? Custom? Social utility? Compelling sentiment? Semi-intuitive apprehension? None of these are likely to be very predictable or reliable. Forget the anxious judge! It is far more anxiety-inducing for parties to lawsuits that a judicial outcome will depend on the sentiments and/or "semi-intuitions" of a given judge on a given day!

Confusing desired outcomes (e.g., "social utility") with justice is the very essence of "siding with the crowd." The "crowd" is the widely-desired outcome. The relevant question then becomes "is it achievable?" rather than "is it right?" This is, unfortunately, what judicial progressivism is about: judges imposing certain desired, "enlightened" outcomes on society. And in contemporary America those desired outcomes are usually the products of postmodern progressive philosophy: once again, the collectivist, "monist" vision of total egalitarianism. The goal is the absolute equality of everything, from economic equality to gender equality to equality of sexual orientation. If there is a distinction, it must be erased. If there is a hierarchy, it must be leveled. The mountains must be brought low and the valleys must be raised. Only then will the utopian vision of progressivism be realized. And if progressives cannot achieve this by persuading their neighbors, they'll shop around for a judge willing to make their neighbors.

So do we need a higher order of justice and morality? Do we really need transcendent standards or have we successfully moved beyond such outdated notions? It is instructive here to return to *The New York Times* editor Bill Keller's op-ed questioning conservative Christian political candidates. While on the one hand he wrote that he didn't care about the specifics of one's religious practices, on the other hand he writes: "I do want to know if a candidate places fealty to the Bible, the Book of Mormon [...] or some other authority higher than the Constitution and laws of this country." In the mind of Keller, having an authority higher than the Constitution and laws of this country is a very bad thing. A simple thought experiment will reveal how ridiculous this is.

Pretend the year is 1860. And pretend that Bill Keller directed this not toward Michele Bachmann or Rick Santorum, but rather to Abraham Lincoln. At the time, remember, the Constitution and laws of this country permitted slavery. Would Keller be concerned that Abraham Lincoln was claiming some extra-Constitutional moral authority to abolish slavery? There were people concerned about that at the time: southern slaveholders. And I, for one, am very glad that Abraham Lincoln derived his moral sense from a higher law than the Constitution and laws of this country. Without that higher authority, the Constitution was an instrument, quite literally, of oppression.

Lincoln certainly would not have thought much of Keller's worries about having some authority higher than the Constitution. And the examples could go on and on. British parliamentarian William Wilberforce fought for the abolition of slavery for decades against the overwhelming odds of "the crowd." Slavery was allowed in British law. Who did he think he was, imposing his sense of morality on people? Or what does Keller make of Martin Luther King, Jr.? Was not the entire Civil Rights movement based on the notion that there is a higher order of justice that America, with her Constitution and laws, was failing to meet?

The progressive notion of justice, one in which there is no higher law than whatever good social ends the State deems necessary to be implemented in the quest for a utopian world of peace and equality, is a tyranny of moral relativism. It is the positive embrace of days of the biblical Judges: "everyone did that which was right in his own eyes" (Judges 21:25). And that doesn't mean everyone does as much evil as possible; it means that they can do evil if deemed necessary. And using justice as a rubber stamp of approval for our desired outcomes is the very essence of what the Bible means by "perverting justice."

---

1. Ross Douthat, "What Has Jerusalem To Do With Athens?" The *New York Times*, May 22, 2012 (http://douthat.blogs.nytimes.com/2012/05/22/what-has-jerusalem-to-do-with-athens/) Emphasis added.

2. Fyodor Dostoevsky, *The Brothers Karamazov*, trans. Constance Garnett (NY: MacMillan, 1922), 701.

3. See his exchanges with Douglas Wilson in their book, *Is Christianity Good For The World?* (Moscow, ID: Canon, 2008), or the documentary based on the book, *Collision* (http://www.collisionmovie.com/)

4. R.R. Reno, "Relativism's Moral Mission," *First Things*, (April 2012), 3.

5. Reno, "Relativism's Moral Mission," 4.

6. "Remarks by the President in Nominating Judge Sonia Sotomayor to the United States Supreme Court," May 26, 2009 (http://www.whitehouse.gov/the_press_office/Remarks-by-the-President-in-Nominating-Judge-Sonia-Sotomayor-to-the-United-States-Supreme-Court)

7. "Sotomayor's 'wise Latina' comment a staple of her speeches," CNN.com (June 5, 2009) (http://articles.cnn.com/2009-06-05/politics/sotomayor.speeches_1_sotomayor-s-confirmation-sotomayor-supporters-judge-sonia-sotomayor?_s=PM:POLITICS)

8. Bradley C. S. Watson, *Living Constitution, Dying Faith—Progressivism and the New Science of Jurisprudence* (Wilmington, DE: ISI Books, advance copy, 2009), 149

CHAPTER EIGHT

ON CRIME & PUNISHMENT

There have been many silly clichés throughout human history, but this one surely must rank as the silliest: "You cannot legislate morality." It is patently nonsensical. The entire point of legislating something, declaring something to be against the law, is to define public morality. The sentiment was invented, of course, by secularists desiring to banish people of religious conviction from the decision-making process about what public morality should be. Even if this exile were successful, it wouldn't make the cliché true. Replacing a public morality based on religious convictions with a public morality justified solely by "secular" principles is still legislating morality. And, as I mentioned previously, the notion that there even are purely secular principles upon which public morality can be based is, at best, highly questionable. Secularists use value-laden terms like human "dignity" and "rights" all the time, but the source of the content filling those words remains something of a mystery. They are empty vessels filled with meaning, or, as Steven Smith puts it, they are mere suitcases in which secularists smuggle their deepest philosophical/

pseudo-religious beliefs into the secular public square. This sleight-of-hand should encourage Christians rather than discourage them. There is no good reason to be intimidated by those insisting that religiously-based moral convictions should be off-limits to public legislation. The reality is that the question is never whether morality should be legislated, but rather whose morality should be legislated.

The idea that the public square should be purely secular has its source in the philosophical movement known as the "Enlightenment." Its rationale is that if people base their convictions on religious grounds there would be no way to get people to agree on public morality. This is because religious convictions tend to be rather intractable and deeply held. The theory is an elegant one: if we can get everybody to lay aside their religious convictions we might have some value-neutral method of garnering widespread public agreement. But the theory is merely that: a theory. The truth is that a purely secular public square is no better at attracting widespread agreement than one in which people openly acknowledge and promote their religious convictions. Ask yourself: when was the last time a significant piece of public legislation affecting some deep moral issue (say, abortion or capital punishment) was passed unanimously? It has, in fact, never happened. The promise that if we all content ourselves with purely secular reasons for public morality then widespread agreement is attainable is a false promise. Devoted as our society is to this principle, it has never actually happened.

An open public square is far more desirable, one in which people can openly acknowledge their deepest convictions (without smuggling them in *via* empty terms) and seek to persuade their neighbors. And evangelical Christians need not smuggle in their deepest convictions. We have a source for morality—the Bible—and there is no reason to be embarrassed about that fact. As much as people cringe in horror at the notion of, say, the Ten Commandments, as we saw in the last chapter that particular code of conduct is not exactly terrifying unless one is committed to, say, murder, theft, and sexual exploitation. But appeal to the Bible as a standard of moral conduct is not without its difficulties. In this chapter we will tackle some of them.

The most foundational question is whether the civil government should be involved in legislating morality in the first place. In chapter five we observed that the primary function of civil government according to the Bible is to adjudicate public morality by rewarding good behavior and punishing evil behavior (Romans 13). "Good" and "evil" are moral terms. According to the Apostle Paul, the civil magistrate is established by God himself as his "minister," an "agent of wrath to bring punishment on the wrongdoer" (Romans 13:4). Criminal justice, the defining and enforcing of public morality, is a divinely-appointed enterprise.

There are a few small segments of the Christian world that do not embrace this teaching and believe that Christians should not involve themselves in matters of judgment (e.g., Anabaptist sects like the Amish or Mennonites). Interestingly, they take this view because of something Paul says immediately prior to Romans 13. He gives personal ethical directives, and among them are these: "Do not repay anyone evil for evil [....] Do not take revenge, my friends, but leave room for God's wrath, for it is written: 'It is mine to avenge; I will repay,' says the Lord" (Romans 12:17-19). This makes it all the more fascinating that, just a few verses later (keep in mind chapters divisions were invented much later) Paul calls the civil magistrate God's *agent of wrath to avenge!* In other words, while individual Christians are not to take revenge, one of the ways God himself takes vengeance on evildoers is precisely by appointing the government to be his servant and to wield "the sword" (Romans 13:4).

Far from something inappropriate for Christians, criminal justice is a high and holy calling!

SIN & CRIME

So the civil government should define and enforce public morality. The question then becomes whose morality? The general sentiment in our culture is that morality should be purely determined by popular vote. We already saw the problem with that in the previous chapter: if there is no higher standard than what the crowd desires, it is a recipe for tyranny and oppression. The strong and powerful (think of early American slaveholders) will legislate to protect their own interests. There must be a higher order of justice that protects the weak and oppressed. This was the rationale of the Civil Rights movement. Popular vote is not enough when it comes to defining and enforcing public morality.

Evangelical Christians should be committed to having the Bible define public morality—after all, civil government is God's servant for the public good. It only makes sense that the servant would take his cues from his master. Indeed, we should be confident in suggesting this because the Western Legal tradition we all take for granted, with its property laws and individual legal protections, is a product of Western Christianity. People did not come up with the ideas of individual human rights to life, liberty, and property by getting rid of Christian moral convictions; they came up with those ideas because of Christian moral convictions. Indeed, some of the greatest legal theorists of all time (e.g., Sir William Blackstone) explicitly based their reasoning on biblical principles of justice.

Does this mean theocracy? That is certainly how it sounds to those who fear the "radical religious Right." It seems incompatible with a classically liberal society based on religious freedom. Doesn't basing public morality on the Bible mean a return to witch trials and executions for heresy? Isn't false religion a crime in the Bible? These are certainly legitimate questions that deserve a thoughtful response.

The first thing to note is that there is a distinction between a sin and a crime. The two often overlap, but not always. In biblical law, for instance, there are all kinds of sins for which God commands his people to repent and offer sacrifices—but for which he never specifies any sort of criminal punishment. The sins of lust, coveting, and hatred are all violations of the Ten Commandments, yet they are not subject to criminal prosecution. When those sins publicly express themselves as sexual assault (lust), theft (coveting), and murder (hatred) they are both sins and crimes, liable to civil punishment. There is a sort of internal/external, private/public distinction involved here: when internal sins outwardly express themselves in actual harm to others (say, assault on a person, theft or destruction of their property) it becomes an issue of public concern. This is consistent with what we found in Romans 13: Paul says the concern of the civil magistrate is outward behavior. The Bible does not endorse the idea of thought crimes, although there are plenty of thought sins. This amounts to a very important restriction on the civil government's jurisdiction and lends solid support to the idea of the freedom of conscience. What a person believes is not a matter of crime. What a person does may very well be a matter of crime. It is worth adding here that progressivism does not provide this sort of fundamental protection—when all that matters is conformity to the collective or the "greater good," what the individual believes becomes a matter of intense scrutiny. "Thought crimes" are part and parcel with the Hegelian ideal manifested in, say, communist societies. This is simply to say that progressivism has its own "theocracy" to be feared; when the State is god, it inevitably punishes heresy.

But there remain difficulties to be resolved. The laws God gave to the Israelites did, in fact, make false worship a crime, not just a sin. Witchcraft and worshiping other gods was punishable by death in ancient Israel. How is this consistent with the distinction between sins and crimes? There is a truly vast amount of literature exploring this question. The historical study of exactly how the largely-Christian West disentangled the church and state and endorsed individual conscience rights, all the while upholding biblical morality, is a huge topic that need not detain us long. But I will briefly explain.

Recall that in the previous chapter we saw that the Ten Commandments are divisible into two categories of law. These are usually called the *first* and *second* "tables" of the law. The first four commandments relate to our duties toward God, and the final six relate to our duties toward others. "You shall have no other gods before me" relates to our direct relationship with God. "You shall not murder" relates to how we act toward other human beings. It is this distinction that explains why Jesus and others summarized the entire law as "loving God and loving our neighbor."

There is a strong case to be made that the first table of the law (our duties toward God) is no longer a matter of crime in the New Testament era (although it certainly remains a matter of sin). In fact, this is by far the majority view among Christian theologians. There are small schools of thought that think differently and, not surprisingly, it is these schools of thought that are hyped by progressives warning against the "dangers" of right-wing theocracy. More particularly, in the latter third of the 20th century there arose a school of thought called Christian Reconstructionism, led largely by Rousas J. Rushdoony, which argued that the entire Mosaic law—first and second tables, case laws, criminal sanctions and all—should be the standard of criminal law for modern nations. Even though Christian Reconstructionism is, by all accounts, a fringe movement (it is even more questionable whether it can even be called a "movement" anymore), that does not stop writers and journalists from trying to associate every Christian politician with the group.[1] Only instead of the parlor game of "Six degrees of Kevin Bacon" it becomes "Six degrees of R. J. Rushdoony." Anyone who knows anyone who read anyone who knows someone who studied Rushdoony… you get the idea. Genuine, true-blue followers of Rushdoony's "theonomic" program are few and far between and hardly worthy of the breathless hysteria emanating from certain quarters.

Here are some of the reasons why many theologians (including me) believe that the Old Testament laws against false worship, while remaining matters of sin, are not matters of crime to be enforced by modern nation-states.

First is the recognition that ancient Israel had a unique place in human history. There are aspects to Israelite society designed to be what theologians call a "type"—a visual illustration of something God was going to fulfill in the future. That future is the final end of all things, wherein God and humanity dwell together in righteousness and peace. The world envisioned is one in which *there is no sin and idolatry*. It was for this typological purpose that God instructed the Israelites to drive the other nations out of the land of Canaan and to publicly enforce their fidelity to God. Other nations did not have this kind of special relationship with God, much less a commission, to establish this sort of society.

Recall that in chapter 3 we saw that Israel's laws were given for different purposes, and it relates directly to this unique calling. Some laws were designed to embody universal moral demands; some were designed as part of the ceremonial system associated with the tabernacle and Temple as visual illustrations of deeper spiritual principles (e.g., blood sacrifice, food laws); and others were historically conditioned sorts of commands, like the mandate to conquer the land of Canaan. These latter two sorts, the "ceremonial" and the historically-conditioned laws, were unique to the people of Israel and not designed to be applied universally. I mentioned that figuring out the purpose of various laws is one of the most difficult tasks in biblical interpretation today. But I believe there are strong indications that the injunctions specifically related to the first table of the law (false worship) are related to Israel's unique calling. The law itself directly relates the admonitions against witchcraft and false worship to Israel's commission to drive out idolatry in Canaan:

> Let no one be found among you who sacrifices his son or daughter in the fire, who practices divination or sorcery, interprets omens, engages in witchcraft, or casts spells, or who is a medium or spiritist or who consults the dead. Anyone who does these things is detestable to the LORD, and because of these detestable practices the LORD your God will *drive out* those nations before you" (Deuteronomy 18:10-12).

Notice to whom this is directed: Israelites. Here, and in the other places where similar injunctions are found, the concern is that the Israelites will not fully cleanse the land of idolatry and will themselves be tempted to follow pagan religion. The moral issue is obeying the command to completely conquer the land of Canaan, which, in the nature of the case, is not a universal moral command (nobody today tries to track down descendants of ancient Canaanites to eradicate them!). This was a task uniquely commanded of ancient Israel, and it visibly foretold of a day where God and his people would dwell together in a land without sin and idolatry (i.e., the new heavens and the new earth).

Further, here is a crucial connection: when God commanded Israel to conquer Canaan he commanded them to "utterly destroy" their enemies—the word in Hebrew is *cherem*, meaning something "devoted to utter destruction" (Joshua 6:17; 1 Samuel 15:21). Important to know is that this directive of *cherem* warfare applied only to Canaanites, not other surrounding nations (Deuteronomy 20:10-18). Treating Canaanite nations as *cherem*, something "devoted to utter destruction," is therefore geographically, historically, and theologically unique. This much is inarguable.

Now, it is immensely significant that the penalty for an individual Israelite (Deuteronomy 7:26) engaged in false, pagan worship or, indeed, an entire Israelite city so engaged (Deuteronomy 13:15) is described as *cherem*: they are to be "devoted to utter destruction." The same word is used. There are no other crimes in biblical law, even death penalty cases, in which the punishment is described using this word. I believe this provides a strong (if not entirely decisive) implication that the laws against false worship in Israel were *a continuing aspect of their conquest of Canaan.* Put another way, these laws ensured that Israel, having entered the land, would not regress and become "Canaanized." And, remarkably, the Bible records later in Judges 20 that Israel actually had need of these laws. The tribe of Benjamin had become so idolatrous and wicked that all Israel went to war with them (with *cherem* as the intent—Judges 20:48!), which was precisely what God commanded them to do in Deuteronomy 13, the very laws against false worship we are considering.

The implication, then, is that Israel's enforcement of the first table of the law is directly related to its unique calling in the conquest of Canaan, and therefore is not reflective of universal principles to be carried out by civil magistrates outside of that unique calling.[2] If *cherem* applied only to Canaanites in the conquest, and to Israelites regressing to Canaanite practices following the conquest, it does not universally apply outside of that unique historical, national, and theological context.

Moreover, in the very context of Romans 13 where the Apostle Paul explains the role of the civil government (which was, at the time, the Roman Empire) and how Christians are to relate publicly with others, he tells them to follow God's moral law. However, he very conspicuously cites only the second table of the law:

> Let no debt remain outstanding, except the continuing debt to love one another, for he who loves his fellowman has fulfilled the law. The commandments, 'Do not commit adultery,' 'Do not murder,' 'Do not steal,' 'Do not covet,' and whatever other commandment there may be, are summed up in this one rule: 'Love your neighbor as yourself.' Love does no harm to its neighbor. Therefore love is the fulfillment of the law (Romans 13:8-10).

Someone will no doubt suggest that I am making an argument from silence—drawing an improper conclusion from what Paul doesn't say. But there is actually more than silence here. It would appear completely inexplicable why he would write that the commandments are "summed up in this *one rule:* love your neighbor as yourself." Literally, it says "summed up in this word" (singular). Every single Jew knew (and knows) that the commandments are summed up in two rules: "Love the Lord your God with all your heart and with all your soul and with all your strength and with all your mind; and, love your neighbor as yourself" (Luke 10:27). The summary of the law is to love God and neighbor. Unless Paul is ignorant of this fact (an absurd suggestion), his sole use of the second table simply has to be purposeful. I see no other plausible explanation. In my view, in Romans 13 Paul is speaking of the *public context subject to the civil authorities,* and he is indicating that only the second table of the law (one's actions toward other people) is relevant to the civil jurisdiction he is addressing.

Finally, Christian theologians wrestling with these issues have universally recognized that Christianity is antithetical to coercion. "Proper belief" is not something achieved by the sword, as it is in other religions one might name. Conversion comes by persuasion and is a work of the Holy Spirit in conjunction with the gospel of grace being preached. The Apostle Paul makes this crystal clear: "For though we live in the world, we do not wage war as the world does. The weapons we fight with are not the weapons of the world" (2 Corinthians 10:3-4). He goes on to identify the gospel message as the weapon that demolishes strongholds, arguments, and pretensions. Joshua destroyed Jericho by *cherem* warfare; Paul destroys strongholds by *preaching.*[3]

CRIME & PUNISHMENT

So there are good reasons to believe that the first table of the law is not the proper jurisdiction of the civil government. One implication is that there is a legitimate, biblical distinction between the church and the state. They are two distinct institutions directed to their own ends. An evangelical theology should not be breezily assumed to entail a "theocracy" because evangelical theology endorses the distinction between church and state. This is not to say that there is a distinction between morality and the state; we have already seen how silly and unworkable that notion is. Even if the realm of beliefs is associated with the independent jurisdictions of the church and/or individual conscience, we are still left with the question of what the jurisdiction of the state is. And the state is instituted by God to define and enforce public morality! So while there should not be "thought" crimes, there certainly are "action" crimes: public moral wrongs. And the state defines and carries out sanctions against these moral wrongs.

In the Bible these "action" crimes are very much the same sorts of action crimes we are concerned about in modern societies: sexual exploitation, theft, vandalism, destruction of property, murder and assault, and so forth. When we focus in on these sorts of crimes in the Bible, we find that they are quite relevant today.[4] While the situational context and the way the law is implemented and enforced may differ for a variety of reasons (e.g., pure historical distance, Israel's unique status), the *moral content* of these laws does, in fact, transcend the horizons of Israel and apply to humanity more generally.

Biblical law is quite unparalleled for its justice and equity. While it might surprise people who instinctively think of biblical law as a relic of more barbaric times, you will not find, for example, penalties like cutting off the hand of a thief. Rather, you will find elaborate schemes to provide restitution for theft (including indentured servitude to pay off the debt). Even in the remarkable Babylonian Code of Hammurabi, which predated the Mosaic code, you will find laws that require different penalties based on socioeconomic status and even death penalties for all sorts of economic crimes like extortion and theft. While Hammurabi taught the principle of *lex talionis* (and "eye for an eye, tooth for tooth"), the practice fell well short of the ideal. The Bible, too, teaches the principle of *lex talionis*, but its consistency is far superior.

Although this principle is basic to the Bible's view of justice—and is therefore one to which evangelical Christians should be thoroughly committed—it is woefully misunderstood today. Many believe that "an eye for an eye, tooth for tooth" is a statement enshrining unjust revenge into the legal code; little could be further from the truth. The point of this legal principle is to mitigate the penalties that can be attached to crimes! It is simply an ancient way of saying "the punishment must fit the crime." It means that a criminal is only liable for the actual damage done, and it therefore protects people from unjust penalties. Cutting off the hand of a thief, for example, violates the principle. If the crime is economic in nature, restitution can and should be arranged.

Even with this in its favor, the truth is that *lex talionis* does enshrine something into the biblical concept of justice that is largely unacceptable to the progressive mind: the principle of *retributive justice*. This is the idea that crime inherently deserves retribution—a payback due to the criminal. When a person lashes out at another and causes harm, the principle of retribution (*lex talionis*) requires that he or she should suffer equal harm as a punishment. This is certainly not a concept currently in vogue, but we abandon it at our peril.

PROGRESSIVISM & CRIME

Part of the progressive project in the 20th century, influenced by the "enlightened" philosophy of utilitarianism, was to discredit the idea of *lex talionis* or retributive justice as barbaric and that it amounts to mere revenge. It is a relic, again, of a Stone Age when people presumed that "two wrongs make a right." What positive good comes from punishing a man simply because he "deserves it"? We must supply more humane and enlightened reasons like, for instance, the rehabilitation of the criminal or the deterrence of others from committing similar crimes. This has clearly been a successful ideological move. Many, if not most, public discussions over criminal law primarily focus on rehabilitation and deterrence. While discussions of public ethics of this kind are often done at high ivory tower levels and we cannot cover all the ground or nuances, we should make a few observations about this progressive trend.

The first thing we must notice is that, once again, the progressive worldview is not at all comfortable with the Bible or the Judeo-Christian tradition. Just as it views the old worldview about human dignity and sexual ethics, property and welfare as archaic museum pieces we must jettison, so also with the old view of justice. It is no longer acceptable to punish a person for a crime because he or she deserves it. On the contrary, the only legitimate reason is for rehabilitation and/or deterrence reasons. This is often deeply intertwined with identity politics as a means of diverting culpability or guilt from the criminal in the first place. Not only is strict retributive justice wrong as a matter of principle, but doubly wrong when one takes into account that the criminal is not likely responsible in the first place! Responsibility lies in poverty, lack of education, poor upbringing, social injustice, and the like.

The great English writer C.S. Lewis once wrote an essay on precisely this topic that has unfortunately never received the attention it properly deserves—and I would partly like to remedy that. The essay is entitled, "The Humanitarian Theory of Punishment."[5] He describes it this way:

> According to the Humanitarian theory, to punish a man because he deserves it, and as much as he deserves, is mere revenge, and, therefore, barbarous and immoral. It is maintained that the only legitimate motives for punishing are the desire to deter others by example or to mend the criminal. When this theory is combined, as frequently happens, with the belief that all crime is more or less pathological, the idea of mending tails off into that of healing or curing and punishment becomes therapeutic. Thus it appears at first sight that we have passed from the harsh and self-righteous notion of giving the wicked their deserts to the charitable and enlightened one of tending the psychologically sick. What could be more amiable?[6]

Lewis's brilliant answer to that question is that the old concept of retributive justice is far and away *more amiable* than this brand-new, shiny, progressive and humane concept of punishment. He begins by making something explicit that is only implicit: "The things done to the criminal, even if they are called cures, will be just as compulsory as they were in the old days when we called them punishments. If a tendency to steal can be cured by psychotherapy, the thief will no doubt be forced to undergo the treatment."[7]

He then lays down the gauntlet: "[T]his doctrine, merciful though it appears, really means that each one of us, from the moment he breaks the law, is deprived of the rights of a human being." In other words, consistent with what we have observed all throughout this book, progressivism has a fundamentally dehumanizing impulse, even in its theory of justice.

I can do no better than to simply summarize Lewis, recognizing that it will barely do him justice. (At some point I think every self-aware Christian writer despairs of communicating as cogently and brilliantly as Lewis.) Readers are greatly encouraged to obtain and read the essay for themselves.

The fundamental reason the humanitarian theory is dehumanizing is that it divorces punishment from what Lewis capitalizes as "Desert." And the concept of Desert is the *only possible link* between punishment and justice. Replacing Desert with therapy, rehabilitation, or deterrence completely undermines justice. It is irrational to speak of a "just cure" or a "just deterrent." We only ask of a cure whether it cures, and of a deterrent whether it deters. And when we no longer ask what a criminal deserves, but replace it with the question of what will cure him or deter others, we remove the criminal from the sphere of justice altogether: "instead of a person, a subject of rights, we now have a mere object, a patient, a 'case.'"

Lewis then asks who is competent to judge such a person. If we follow the new progressive model of justice, "the only two questions we may now ask about a punishment are whether it deters and whether it cures." And those are not questions for people trained in jurisprudence, rights, and duties:

> Only the expert 'penologist' (let barbarous things have barbarous names), in the light of previous experiment, can tell us what is likely to deter: only the psychotherapist can tell us what is likely to cure. It will be in vain for the rest of us, speaking simply as men, to say, 'but this punishment is hideously unjust, hideously disproportionate to the criminal's deserts.' The experts with perfect logic will reply, 'but nobody was talking about deserts. No one was talking about punishment in your archaic vindictive sense of the word. Here are the statistics proving that this treatment deters. Here are the statistics proving that this treatment cures. What is your trouble?[8]

We can now begin to see more clearly where this leads: the humanitarian theory "removes sentences from the hands of jurists whom the public conscience is entitled to criticize and places them in the hands of technical experts whose special sciences do not even employ such categories as rights or justice." This is a recipe for complete tyranny. Keep in mind that the "cure" or the "deterrent" is just as compulsory as the older concept of "punishment." The language is more soothing, surely, but Lewis warns not to be deceived by names:

> To be taken without consent from my home and friends; to lose my liberty; to undergo all those assaults on my personality which modern psychotherapy knows how to deliver; to be re-made after some pattern of 'normality' hatched in a Viennese laboratory to which I never professed allegiance; to know that this process will never end until either my captors have succeeded or I grow wise enough to cheat them with apparent success—who cares whether this is called Punishment or not? That it includes most of the elements for which

any punishment is feared—shame, exile, bondage, and years eaten by the locust—is obvious. Only enormous ill-desert could justify it; but ill-desert is the very conception which the Humanitarian theory has thrown overboard.[9]

If I could, I would simply reproduce the entire essay because it delves into the delicate question of Christianity and the public square. But I will close with this observation. Lewis says the real practical problem of Christian politics is not really fashioning blueprints for the just society, but learning to live our lives under unbelieving rulers who are often "very wicked and very foolish."

> And when they are wicked the Humanitarian theory of punishment will put in their hands a finer instrument of tyranny than wickedness ever had before. For if crime and disease are to be regarded as the same thing, it follows that any state of mind which our masters choose to call 'disease' can be treated as a crime; and compulsorily cured.[10]

Thus it is that a progressive view of justice that claims to have transcended the old, vindictive concept of *lex talionis* in actuality dispenses with the concept of justice altogether and substitutes tyrannical euphemisms in its place. Lewis writes, "[T]o be punished, however severely, because we have deserved it, because we 'ought to have known better,' is to be treated as a human person made in God's image." The alternative is dehumanizing. It is yet another "magic formula" whereby the State can punish dissidents with impunity all under the banner of being "compassionate." Is this not exactly what takes place in communist societies? And is it not alarming that certain people in our society—say, conservative evangelical Christians—are routinely depicted as crazy or mentally ill when they oppose the inexorable expansion of the State into every nook and cranny of life? Lewis was perfectly right to fear an all-powerful State armed with the "humanitarian" theory of punishment. It is a fine instrument of tyranny, indeed. The biblical concept of justice, *lex talionis*, "an eye for an eye, tooth for tooth," is an essential and indispensable element of a truly free society. Progressivism rejects this concept of justice, and will lose free society along with it.

---

1. For a particularly egregious example, see Ryan Lizza, "Leap of Faith: The Making of a Republican Frontrunner" *The New Yorker*, August 15, 2011 (http://www.newyorker.com/reporting/2011/08/15/110815fa_fact_lizza); and Joe Carter's response, "A Journalism Lesson for the New Yorker," *First Things*, August 10, 2011 (http://www.firstthings.com/onthesquare/2011/08/a-journalism-lesson-for-the-new-yorker)

2. Although I will not deal with it directly here since I find it less a priority than the question of religious crimes, many offer credible arguments along similar lines that some of the *criminal sanctions* of biblical law are likewise unique to Israel's status as a theocratic society.

3. For readers interested in digging deeper, I recommend Vern S. Poythress, *The Shadow of Christ in the Law of Moses* (Phillipsburg: Presbyterian & Reformed, 1995)

4. For a recent and magisterial look at biblical law from the perspective of a modern lawyer, see Jonathan Burnside, *God, Justice, & Society* (Oxford: Oxford University Press, 2010)

5. C.S. Lewis, "The Humanitarian Theory of Punishment," in *God in the Dock: Essays on Theology and Ethics* (Grand Rapids: Eerdmans, reprint 2001), 287-300. (This can also be found online at http://www.angelfire.com/pro/lewiscs/humanitarian.html)

6. Lewis, "Humanitarian Theory," 287-8.

7. Lewis, "Humanitarian Theory," 288.

8. Lewis, "Humanitarian Theory," 289.

9. Lewis, "Humanitarian Theory," 290-91.

10. Lewis, "Humanitarian Theory," 293.

CHAPTER NINE

ON JUST WAR

I began the last chapter by calling the cliché "You cannot legislate morality" arguably the silliest in human history. Giving it at least a very close run for the prize is the one emblazoned on a bumper sticker: "Make love, not war." This cliché has the wonderful advantage (not least because of its money-making implications) of having a thousand permutations: "Make art, not war," "Make jobs, not war," "Make tea, not war." War, it seems, can be simply replaced with anything benign or well-meaning. I admit that it would be a wonderful world if sex was a real alternative to war. Unfortunately, we do not live in a land of unicorns and fairies. I prefer another bumper sticker I saw recently:

> Except for ending slavery, Fascism, Nazism, and Communism, war has never solved anything.

It is not a full-fledged promotion of war, exactly. It is a promotion of war in certain circumstances. And that is exactly what I believe an evangelical theology should endorse: war *in certain circumstances*.

What those circumstances are can be tricky, of course. For that reason I believe that this issue, above all the others I've treated in this book, leaves the most room for disagreement among evangelical Christians. I will not be so presumptuous as to make determinations about the propriety of the various recent wars America has engaged in, whether in Iraq, Afghanistan, or Libya. What I am concerned about, however, is the more foundational issue of whether war itself is ever justified and necessary.

In keeping with its vision of heaven on earth, progressivism has always had as a primary goal the eradication of war. America's first self-consciously Hegelian President, Woodrow Wilson, helped found the League of Nations in the early 20th century to facilitate the day when Isaiah's prophecy would be fulfilled ahead of schedule and all "the swords would be beaten into plowshares" (Isaiah 2:4). The result left so much to be desired that the League of Nations quickly outlived its usefulness. This mainly had to do with Germany's insistence in 1939 on repeating the horrific catastrophe of the First World War. However, as soon as the second global conflagration ended with the surrender of Japan in 1945, a new parliament of humanity was organized under the banner of the United Nations. The goal of the United Nations is, according to the preamble to its charter, "to save succeeding generations from the scourge of war, which twice in our lifetime has brought untold sorrow to mankind."

If judged by this purpose, it must be said that the United Nations, like its forerunner, has been an abject failure. Yes, we have been saved from worldwide conflicts engulfing all continents, but this has more to do with the advent of the nuclear weapon than the good intentions of diplomats. In the 1960s progressivism's anti-war platform was rejuvenated by student riots and demonstrations against the Vietnam conflict, and it is safe to say that antipathy to war is fairly well-embedded into the DNA of modern progressivism (except, of course, when progressive politicians engage in war; then it becomes a grudging necessity about which a polite silence is maintained). Recalling Thomas Sowell's question of why it is always the same people lined up on opposite sides of completely different issues, we should wonder: when progressives demonstrate against corporate America or the greed of Wall Street, why is it always simultaneously an antiwar rally? You will never see a progressive rally without a "No blood for oil!" sign or something similar. Once again, it is because the issues are not unrelated. The background worldview of progressivism binds seemingly diverse interests together.

When progressives stick "Visualize World Peace" on their vehicles, they are visualizing nothing less than a utopian heaven on earth, and this heaven on earth encompasses the entire array of human endeavors, from morality ("My Body, My Choice!") to economics ("People, Not Profits!") to war ("Peace, Not War!"). Moreover, they believe all this is actually achievable, though if pressed they would probably admit that it isn't really done by visualizing, making love, or drinking tea. The unconstrained vision of progressive utopianism is what underlies the antiwar movement, and it is encapsulated again by John Lennon's *Imagine*: a world where there is "nothing to kill or die for." This is the ideology of pacifism, making peace a supreme virtue to be pursued at all costs. And as much as I might try, along with Lennon, I have a difficult time imagining and getting excited about a world in which there is "nothing to die for." It sounds very much like a world where nothing can be truly loved.

CHRISTIAN PACIFISM?

There have always been minority groups within Christianity that also embrace pacifism as an ideology. No matter the reason and no matter how noble the goals, they believe Christians should be against war in all circumstances. War in its essence is the exercise of violence and power, two things that should be renounced by followers of Jesus. In America this sort of Christian pacifism is most closely associated with Anabaptist groups like the Amish or Mennonites, and exemplified in the writings of influential theologians like John Howard Yoder and Stanley Hauerwas.[1]

In evaluating Christian pacifism it is helpful first to reflect on the peculiar fact that it has always been a decidedly minority view in history. It is possible, I suppose, that the vast majority of Christians in the past 2,000 years have simply misunderstood the ethic of Jesus or failed to comprehend its true meaning—possible, but hardly probable. This basic maneuver is characteristic of Anabaptist theology more generally. Anabaptism was the "radical" or "left wing" of the Protestant Reformation, and one of its defining features is the critique that mainstream Protestantism did not go nearly far enough in breaking with its catholic past. Whereas the Lutherans and Calvinists wanted to maintain their true continuity with the historical church, Anabaptists insisted on complete discontinuity, as if the truth had been lost for centuries and only in the 16th century recovered anew. This contrarian ethos has infused Anabaptist theology ever since, and explains why Christian pacifists are undeterred by the fact that few in the history of the church have embraced their views. They have no problem saying that everybody has been wrong for thousands of years. They really ought to have a problem saying that.

The animating principle of Christian pacifism—the *sina qua non,* the one thing it cannot do without—is the conviction that violence and power are intrinsically evil and contrary to the way of God. In their reading, Jesus' instructions in the Sermon on the Mount not to repay evil for evil and to "turn the other cheek" entail a wholesale commitment to nonviolent resistance. It is this teaching, to "love one's enemies," which forms Jesus' most decisive and revolutionary break with the patterns of this world (and surely there is an element of truth to this). In their view this aspect of Jesus' teaching was, in fact, the arrival of the Kingdom of God. Doctrine, dogma, theology, creeds, confessions, institutions—these are all ancillary at best to the heart of genuine Christianity. The heart of Christianity is an ethic: the "Way of Peace," which is the absolute commitment to nonviolence.

As will become abundantly clear in a moment, as a theologian I believe this is nonsense. But I want to add this: Anabaptists have not chosen this path because it is easy. One can laugh, I suppose, at the person who refuses to defend himself in the face of violence. One can find it absurd that a person would renounce the right of self-defense. Anabaptists have never lived in the lap of luxury; they have had a very difficult time of it in the world. They have been exiled, intensely persecuted, burned at the stake, and utterly scorned by the world for their beliefs. Yes, the theology might be deficient, but there is something here worthy of admiration. And I believe that often that something is a sincere love of Jesus and convicted conscience. One may suffer the wrath of the world for the name of Jesus unnecessarily, as I believe is the case here, but it is suffering for the name of Jesus, nonetheless.

Having made this decision to prioritize the "Way of Peace" in this manner, all else in the Bible is subordinated to it. Theologians call this having a "canon within a canon," and it is very similar to what we saw when President Obama contrasted an "obscure line in Romans" with the Sermon on the Mount. One part of the "canon" of Scripture (Sermon on the Mount) becomes a prioritized, higher authority over the rest of Scripture (say, Romans). The "Way of Peace" as the pacifist reads it becomes a higher norm than the rest of the Bible itself. I view this as essentially a denial of the unity of the Bible for the simple reason that the rest of the Bible does not support a pacifist reading of the Sermon on the Mount.

I touched on this, in fact, at the beginning of the previous chapter, and it is worth circling back around to it. In Romans 12 Paul explicitly reiterates Jesus' commands to not repay evil for evil and to not take vengeance. And yet, just a few verses later he endorses the civil magistrate as a God-ordained institution that avenges by executing wrath on the wrongdoer. Indeed, he even says that the magistrate "bears the sword." That is a rather violent image. Paul's reading of the Sermon on the Mount, at least, does not entail the complete renunciation of all violence as evil. On the contrary, the civil magistrate is uniquely established by God to exact vengeance on wrongdoers. The distinction is simply one of *spheres of jurisdiction.* Paul's reiteration of Jesus' pronouncements in the Sermon on the Mount indicates that Christians, as individuals, or even together as an organized church, are not to seek revenge, but rather to repay evil with good. Unless this distinction is in mind, then we arrive at the truly grotesque prospect of the civil authorities themselves repaying evil with good. "Commit murder? Good. Freedom for you!" This is exactly the opposite of what Paul has just suggested as the purpose for civil government: to reward good and punish evil.

The problem is the root principle that all violence is evil, something completely unworthy of God and therefore incompatible with the "way of God." It is this assumption that not only renders Paul's teaching on the civil government in Romans 13 unintelligible, but it makes the rest of the Bible obscure beyond your wildest imagination. A number of years ago in postgraduate school I attended a seminar in which one of the world's leading Mennonite scholars (it is, admittedly, a small club) presented a paper: Thomas N. Finger, author of *A Contemporary Anabaptist Theology: Biblical, Historical, Constructive.*[2] Dr. Finger sat around a conference table with a few university faculty members and a dozen or so postgraduate students and presented a paper. His purpose was to attempt to reconcile the Mennonite pacifist "Way of Peace" with the entire rest of the Bible. I commend Dr. Finger for undertaking the project. At very least, he sensed that if the principle of nonviolent resistance is to be a truly Christian doctrine it must fit with the entirety of Christian Scripture. This is a daunting and, as we were to discover in the seminar, a literally impossible task.

Dr. Finger spent an hour or so working his way through the Bible and all the instances in which it portrays God as participating in violence, each time suggesting extremely contorted interpretations designed to essentially get God "off the moral hook." Of course, it is only a "moral hook" if violence *equals* evil. The students were, to put it mildly, utterly incredulous. That time God destroyed the entire world with a flood? Not God engaged in violence. That time God commanded the Israelites to utterly destroy the Canaanites? Not God engaged in violence. And so on.

The time for entertaining questions arrived, and he was asked about a variety of other problematic biblical texts, including one from me about the book of Revelation, which portrays Jesus as a triumphant King who brings wrath down on his enemies. Given the situation and position he was defending, Dr. Finger did an adequate job deflecting. In fact, he had answers (not necessarily good ones) for every question. Finally, after the better part of an hour, a gentleman who happens to be one of the world's most renowned theologians finally stumped him. He very politely inquired (and I am paraphrasing by memory): "But Tom, what about the cross? If God is not doing *violence* to his Son, if the cross is not God's full and final 'No!' to evil, then what is left of Christianity?" It left Dr. Finger completely at a loss for words as the implications sank in. Equating violence with evil ultimately undermines the central event of

Christianity: God violently pouring out judgment and wrath on his Son in the place of sinful humanity.

This is one reason why the majority of Christians throughout history have refused to make this equation, sentimental and tempting as it seems. There is evil in the world and until the time when he finally eradicates it at the final judgment, God has instituted ways of mitigating—even combatting—evil. The means he has appointed is the civil government, who uniquely "bears the sword" as an "agent of wrath to bring punishment on the evildoer" (Romans 13:4). This certainly means that criminal justice, with its police force and court systems, is God-ordained and legitimate in dealing with domestic evil. But it also means that waging war can be legitimate in dealing with foreign evil.

THE REALITY OF EVIL

Here is a basic fact: there are evildoers in the world. Basic to Christian theology is the understanding that human beings are fallen. They are capable of engaging in horrific acts of evil, and this cannot be doubted by anyone who has been alive for more than a few minutes. G. K. Chesterton once humorously quipped that the doctrine of original sin is "the only part of Christian theology that can really be proved." The fallen character of humanity is what leads to the occasional necessity of war. Think of it: if God truly loves human beings and desires their prosperity in the world, as I have argued in this book, then it is quite unthinkable that God turns a blind eye to evildoers seeking to do harm to people and their prosperity. One of the ways God has established to restrain and mitigate the evils of some is to appoint the civil government to punish evil and to protect the lives and livelihood of the people entrusted to their care. The state, as Paul says, "does not bear the sword in vain." Militaries designed to protect people from foreign assault is just as legitimate and God-ordained as the local police force.

Progressivism, on the other hand, does not have the advantage of having a consistent view of human nature. Chesterton notwithstanding, they are not at all convinced of original sin and the reality of evil in the world. After all, the goal is to inaugurate utopian peace and prosperity, a "brotherhood of man" sharing the entire world. Evil is not part of human nature this side of the fall; it is something that can be transcended in the here-and-now because human nature is basically good. If it sometimes falls short of this goodness it is nevertheless malleable; it can be reprogrammed. The progressive utopian dream rests on an unconstrained view of humanity, and that entails that humanity is not basically evil.

This is why progressives habitually talk about global conflicts as problems of misunderstanding. Following the World Trade Center attacks in September of 2001, the knee-jerk response was: "Why do they hate us?" As though A) there is some legitimate reason for incinerating 3,000 innocent people; and B) it all rests on some failure of comprehension. As Michael Moore lamented in the hours following the atrocity, don't they know that New York didn't *vote for Bush?* Yes, had they only known better, had they merely checked the Electoral College map of the year 2000, al-Qaeda surely would have scrapped the mission. This is not to mention that Moore implies that people who "voted for Bush" would have deserved incineration. This is a stark reminder of what I called the xenophobia of progressivism: anyone not with the program is "other."

This Pollyanna view of the human nature is also why progressivism is so enamored with diplomacy. Every threat can be overcome by talking because our enemies are rational—indeed, morally good—actors. It is what Chamberlain thought of Hitler, the progressive left thought of

Soviet leadership, and what many believe about the Mullahs of Iran today. I realize that progressives style their views of diplomacy and international affairs as pragmatic "realism." But there is nothing realistic about a view of human nature that discounts the reality that some people are very, very evil.

It is more complicated than this, however. While on the one hand they have a sunny optimism about human nature, on the other hand the progressive antiwar movement does seem to believe in various incarnations of evil: George W. Bush is evil, the American "military-industrial complex" is evil, neo-colonialism is evil, "blood for oil is evil," and the list goes endlessly on. Everything on the "evil" list is something America is or something America (or its allies) does. What progressivism lacks (not surprisingly, given its inherent moral relativism) is a consistent view of human nature and a principled way of analyzing moral and immoral actions. When Hamas blows up a busy pizza parlor using a suicide bomber, this is justifiable and legitimate as "blowback" for the misdeeds of America and Israel. This same analysis never applies in the other direction, even though America and Israel would never dream of using suicide bombers to attack unsuspecting civilians.

JUST WAR THEORY

Christian theology, armed with a realistic view of human nature, has recognized that not everybody is a morally good and rational actor. It knows that many of the problems that precipitate war are deeply ethical and moral failures rather than merely failures of understanding and comprehension. Put simply, war is not only sometimes necessary; sometimes it is the only moral course of action. The civil government has the moral duty to protect its citizens from attack, and sometimes this can only be done with military action.

Given this recognition, Christian theologians and moral philosophers for the better part of two millennia have explored the ethics of war. They developed an entire tradition of careful moral thinking that goes far beyond the simplistic pragmatism evident in much progressive (and some neo-conservative) thinking today. This is the tradition of "Just War Theory." In addition to reflecting on what sorts of moral reasons are legitimate for *entering* a war (*jus ad bellum*), they carefully considered what *kinds* of warfare are ethical (*jus in bello*). Put in modern terms, the Just War tradition contemplates "war-decision law" (when to enter a conflict) and "war-conduct law" (how to fight once in a conflict). Here are some of the moral principles:

1. The cause for war must itself be just: correcting a suffered wrong, protecting human lives in imminent danger, or correcting grave, public evil. A war is not just if its purpose is simply expand territory or to increase economic gain.

2. The purpose of war must be the restoration of ordered peace.

3. War can only be initiated by legitimate civil authorities, not vigilantes or private armies.

4. War is a last resort, to be initiated only after peaceful alternatives have been shown non-viable; this should not mean that a nation can simply engage in never-ending negotiations as a way of avoiding war.

5. There must be a probability of success. Throwing combatants into a war of futility is immoral.

6. There must be proportionality between the expected benefits of war and its expected evils and harms.

Applying these principles to real-world situations is a difficult task, and reasonable people can and do disagree about specific applications. But disagreement does not make the principles worthless. Imagine how much more difficult (and unjust!) it would be without this kind of moral guidance. There would be no restraint on civil authorities at all, only their private, pragmatic intuitions.

Many people lament that the Just War tradition has fallen on hard times, especially with the policies of "preemptive" war pursued by the George W. Bush administration or even recent military intervention for strictly humanitarian purposes. I understand that concern. But I would argue that the very fact that the Bush administration had to provide elaborate rationales for its concept of preemptive war (e.g., the new reality of global terrorist networks, the nexus between terrorism and weapons of mass destruction) actually indicates that the Just War tradition is alive and well. Nobody suggests that the government can go to war for any and every reason. Imperfect as it may be, the Christian Just War tradition does, in fact, provide restraints even on the American Empire.

The Just War tradition also supplies ethical norms for how actual combatants should engage in warfare. Some of them include:

1. A distinction must be made and maintained between combatants and non-combatants. Only the former are legitimate targets of force.

2. There must be a principle of proportionality. Military action should not be unnecessarily destructive, but should use the amount of force necessary to achieve the objective. Using a nuclear bomb to sabotage an airfield, for example, would be grossly disproportionate.

3. Related to the principle of proportionality, there should be a principle of minimum force as a means to limit unnecessary death and destruction.

The rules for *jus ad bellum* provide restraints on civil governments when it comes to entering a war, and the rules for *jus in bello* provide restraints for actual combatants. The actual history of how these rules have been applied or not applied is a messy one. Humanity, remember, is fallen and constrained. We often fall short of our ideals. For example, I believe the targeted bombing of civilization populations in World War II clearly failed the principles of the just conduct of war.

I just mentioned that there are actually encouraging signs when it comes to the viability of the Just War tradition—namely, the fact that American administrations explicitly recognize the need to morally justify its wars. The alternative is not very attractive. But I believe there are even more encouraging signs when it comes to the actual conduct of war. The truth is that no empire in the history of the world has done more to conduct wars in a just and moral way than the United States of America. No nation has equaled its efforts to develop technologies and weaponry specifically designed to *mitigate unnecessary casualties.* A "smart" bomb dropped from twenty thousand feet that enters *this* window and not *that* window is a moral advance in the nature of war. When American soldiers are caught mistreating prisoners (Abu Ghraib), murdering non-combatants, or desecrating bodies, they are court-martialed and imprisoned. Alexander the Great had no such moral sensitivities. In fact, it can even be argued that the American military is too morally circumspect when it comes to waging war when it imposes extremely burdensome rules of engagement on its soldiers.

Just War theory is not a science; it is moral art. Application of its principles tends toward the gray part of the color spectrum instead of black and white. But what is black and white, in my estimation, is that war is not inherently evil. God appointed civil rulers to protect their citizens, and therefore war can be the moral course of action.

Evangelical theology endorses the role of the civil government in waging war. It recognizes the reality that there is evil in the world that must be opposed. It knows that violence is not identical to evil. Therefore, evangelicals should not be pacifists. To turn the discussion to the political arena, while there are those on the right wing of American politics who are altogether too glib about military intervention (and we should be wary of them), the truth is that full-fledged pacifism, at least since the rise of the antiwar left in the 1960s, is far more associated with the progressivism of the left wing. Pacifism rooted in progressivism's rosy view of humanity's inherent goodness and the hope of a this-worldly utopia of tolerance, understanding, peace, and prosperity is a positively dangerous thing.

Because the rosy view is wrong.

---

1. John Howard Yoder, *The Politics of Jesus* (Grand Rapids: Eerdmans, reprint 1994); Stanley Hauerwas, *War & The American Difference: Theological Reflections on Violence and National Identity* (Grand Rapids: Baker, 2011).

2. Thomas N. Finger, *A Contemporary Anabaptist Theology: Biblical, Historical, Constructive* (Downer's Grove: InterVarsity, 2004)

CONCLUSION

God loves people.

God loves prosperity.

God loves justice.

This book has explored these three biblical themes and how they relate the contemporary political issues. God's love of these things is rooted in his very character. It is *this* God, the one who loves people, prosperity, and justice, who created all things. More specifically, God created human beings to reflect and image him by loving the things he loves.

For human society to love people as God loves them means that it must prioritize the protection of human life from beginning to end. It must recognize the intrinsic dignity and value of every human being. It must protect the institutional design for human flourishing: marriage between one man and one woman.

For human society to love prosperity as God loves it means that it must protect the rights of private property and preserve the economic incentives established in the creational mandate of work and reward.

For human society to love justice as God loves it means that it must recognize that this is a morally-ordered universe and that there is a law above the law. Justice cannot be a respecter of persons by being mixed with identity politics. Justice must be blindfolded and committed to the concept of retribution. Without it the tie between punishment and justice is undermined and tyranny reigns. Society must further recognize that justice requires the civil government to protect its people from foreign enemies and that sometimes war is a moral course of action.

I believe all these convictions flow from an evangelical theology, and I further believe these convictions are essential to a free and virtuous society. We have discovered throughout this book, however, that this vision for society, this worldview, is at odds with modern political progressivism from start to finish. Progressivism does not believe there is a creational design. There is no God who loves anything. Reality has no built-in hardware; it is all reprogrammable software. Human nature can be refashioned, if we would only imagine it. It is "easy if you try."

Progressivism desires to progress beyond the old, archaic worldview of Christianity. This has been its goal since the French revolution, and it has been explicitly advocated by philosophers and political theorists ever since. Collective humanity, embodied in the State, is the god who will replace the true Creator of heaven and earth. We will create our own destiny. We will progress beyond the creational structures and inaugurate a "new heavens and new earth" right here and right now.

The only trouble is that every single attempt so far to create this heaven on earth has ended in a living hell. This is because reality does not match the progressive "magic formulas." There are creational designs for human flourishing, and rejecting them produces the opposite of flourishing.

I know that many Americans are deeply cynical about politics. There is much, I admit, to discourage us. Politicians can be unprincipled and corrupt. Partisan politics as waged in the age of a 24/7 news cycle and cable network shows is sometimes unimaginably banal. But we need to remember afresh how extremely blessed we are to live in a land where our participation is welcomed at the ballot box. We forget that this privilege has been experienced by very few human beings in the history of the world.

Cynicism is not an option for the evangelical Christian who truly believes in God and his designs for human flourishing. Throwing up our hands in disgust while we have hands to serve or retreating to our ghettos when the public square is open for business is a lack of thankfulness to the God we profess.

My purpose has been to expose the broader ideological background behind the partisan divide in America. I began by saying that I do not believe politics to be all that complicated, and I maintain that view especially now at the end of this book. I believe progressivism is essentially anti-Christian both in its historical origin and contemporary articulation. I often hear evangelicals say things like, "Conservatives are good on pro-life issues, but liberals are better on social justice issues." If I have accomplished anything, I hope it is to convince you that this is not even remotely the trade-off. I cannot, in fact, think of a single area treated in this book where progressivism has turned out to have a program that leads to human flourishing or a free and virtuous society.

I do not want to render this book inherently dated by talking specifically about any particular election. But I do think a few general observations about the moment in which we find ourselves are appropriate. I know evangelical Christians who are fed up with the two-party system and are convinced that there is no discernible difference between the two. They believe that American decline is inevitable, and voting the Republican ticket simply delays the decline. This point of view requires, unfortunately, a healthy measure of arrogance. Think about it: this view claims to know the course of the future. It claims to know what is "inevitable." It claims to know what historical forces can or cannot be stopped. It claims to know that the slope is so slippery that our downward regress cannot be impeded. It claims to know, in other words, things that God has not deigned to share with us. I find great wisdom in Jonah Goldberg's admonition:

> So long as one remembers that the slippery slope isn't a *thing* but a metaphor, it's not so bad. It's when people believe that it describes an actual phenomenon, a mechanism of historical progression, that the slippery slope becomes an invitation to surrender. If you take it as a given that losing an inch means you've already lost the mile, then you will give up after losing the inch. That is precisely what the other side wants you to do: give up prematurely. If you go through life thinking the slippery slope is real, you will make it real. If you go through life a happy warrior, believing every good fight is worth having because it is good, and every defeat is temporary, you might have other problems, but you won't have the problem of premature capitulation.[1]

A cynical "they're all the same" attitude lacks perspective in other ways. It suffers from the problem that "they" are not all the same. In the United Kingdom conservatives get to vote for candidates who are very liberal by American standards: in favor of abortion, for same-sex "marriage," champions of a welfare state (just a "smarter" welfare state, mind you). There is depressingly little difference between, say, Tony Blair and David Cameron. With that in mind, the two-party system in America blessedly does not simply represent strong and weak versions of the same political agenda.

In the upcoming 2012 elections, the incumbent party promises a progressive platform of abortion-on-demand and same-sex marriage, contrary to God's designs for life and sexuality. They promise higher taxes and wealth redistribution, as well as a never-ending expansion of the welfare state, contrary to God's designs for private property and genuine charity. They promise identity politics and legal favoritism based on race, gender, class, and sexual orientation, contrary to God's design that justice be blindfolded.

The other party's platform takes the opposing view on every issue. So I will end right where I began: I do not believe that it is all that complicated.

---

1.   Jonah Goldberg, *The Tyranny of Clichés*, 120.

ACKNOWLEDGEMENTS

Thanks to God, Father, Son, and Holy Spirit for creating me and saving me.

Thanks to all my girls, for making my life worth living.

Thanks to my colleagues, Andrew, Jeff, and David, for the encouragement and the platform.

Thanks to Susan and Amy for the proofreading.

Thanks to Jeremiah for the quiet space and the trout stream.

Thanks to Casey and Preacherboy's Draught Room for friendship (and beer).

Thanks to Off The Leaf Coffee Bar for the Americanos.

Thanks to everyone involved in making the conservative movement in America stronger than it has been in generations. I cannot name everyone, but here is the top of my list: Alan Sears and the Alliance Defense Fund, The Acton Institute, The Heritage Foundation, Rush Limbaugh, Hugh Hewitt, *National Review, The Weekly Standard,* and *Powerline.* Finally, thanks to civic leaders who embody a genuine love of people, prosperity, and justice.

ABOUT THE AUTHOR

Brian G. Mattson, B.A., M.A.R., Ph.D. (University of Aberdeen), is Senior Scholar of Public Theology for the Center For Cultural Leadership (WWW.CHRISTIANCULTURE.COM). He is author of *Restored To Our Destiny*, an academic monograph on the theology of noted 19th century Dutch theologian Herman Bavinck. In addition to being a theologian, he has an alter-ego who moonlights as a musician and singer/songwriter. He resides in his hometown of Billings, Montana, with his wife and two daughters. He blogs at WWW.DRBRIANMATTSON.COM, and his Twitter handle is @BrianGMattson.

Made in the USA
Middletown, DE
30 March 2024